Suicide & Sequins

A Journey of Joyous Hope

Jenny DeBolt

Published by Lemonade Legend Publishing

Trigger Warning

This book contains descriptions of suicide, grief, alcoholism, and mental illness.

Suicide Hotlines in The United States

Crisis Text Line	Text HOME to 741741
National Suicide Prevention Lifeline	1-800-273-8255
Veterans Crisis Line	1-800-273-8255, Press 1
Transgender Lifeline	1-877-565-8860
Trevor Lifeline	1-866-488-7386 (for LGBTQ youth)

Disclaimer

This book is not intended as a substitute for the medical and psychological advice of a licensed clinician, physician, therapist, or psychiatrist. The author is not a licensed professional. The content of this book is for informational purposes only and is not intended to diagnose, treat, cure, or prevent any clinical condition or state of mind. Please consult with your own professional regarding the suggestions and recommendations in this book.

DEDICATION

I lovingly dedicate this book to the men in my life. My husband, Mike DeBolt, and my sons, Cody Gibson, and Brady Gibson. They loved me when I felt unlovable. They loved me when I neglected them during my grief. They loved me when I withdrew from actively loving them. They did all of this while grieving themselves. I do not even have words to express my gratitude for their selflessness. They literally saved my life, and they won't know that until they read this dedication.

That's the thing about grief. We hide it so we can fit in with the normalcy surrounding us even though we feel far from normal. People are going on with their lives and we that are grieving feel left behind. So, we pretend everything is fine when around the seemingly normal people. When we are alone, some of our actions are far from fine. We have a complete breakdown in our fundamental life duties like brushing our teeth or bathing. We don't even really care. At times, we quite literally smell from our lack of basic selfcare. We don't even notice. We are too tied up in our emotional trauma from grief to bother with a sense like smell.

Mike, Cody, and Brady made me feel a little normal everyday with their love. With their acceptance. With their mere presence. They helped me see that I still fit in. I love all of you with every essence of my being.

Table of Contents

Foreword

I'll never forget meeting Jenny for the first time. When Jenny walks into a room, regardless of the setting, people notice. She's bright (literally), she's pink, and her lips turn up at either end.

Even in a stale room, with generic folding chairs, set up in a circle for a grief support group. Jenny's image defies what mourning "should" look like. It's also a stark reminder that grief has no "look" and trauma doesn't just strike the downtrodden.

Suicide is an unimaginable ending to someone's life. It's often hard to explain, and commonly misunderstood. For these reasons, those who are left behind, known as Survivors of Suicide (SOS), are left to grieve alone. Or at least that is how they perceive it. Stop and ask yourself, how often have you been impacted by suicide before now? Maybe you have never been impacted by suicide. What was the first suicide you remember hearing about in your life? How old were you? How did the people around you respond to this loss? Did they sit you down and explain it, or at least try? Or was it mentioned once, maybe even with some judgment, and then swept under the rug and not really addressed again? Many of those scenarios are what we are familiar with. It's what society has modeled for us. No wonder Survivors of Suicide feel alone. Those around them have not been taught how to give them support. Maybe they have even been taught to believe that the act of suicide is shameful and selfish.

I've spent a great portion of my life working with individuals suffering from a loss to suicide. Twenty years of my life exactly. What I have always said is that most of my knowledge has come from those who were grieving. I didn't learn about suicide in graduate school, well, not more than a few hours. I don't consider that "learning." No scholarly book prepared me to work with those bereaved by suicide. Instead, I learned by diving in! Sitting in that support group circle I described above. Anything of value that I have learned about suicide grief I have learned from walking alongside hundreds, if not thousands, of loved ones that are just trying to breathe and make logical sense out of an illogical act. Survivors have taught me how lonely it can be. Survivors have taught me how confusing, desperate, and depressing it can be. Survivors have taught me that even after struggling to survive this catastrophic loss, they too, can contemplate suicide. That seems so *ironic,* doesn't it?

I've also been honored to read journals of those who have died by suicide. I have been entrusted by surviving family members with the pages of their loved ones' most intimate thoughts, and sometimes the nonsensical loops of irrational themes that bring these individuals to believe that life can never be better. I've been trained by experts in the field of suicidology and recently have dug deeper into understanding the suicidal mind. The hope in continuing to learn is simple—it's to help a Survivor understand.

Those left behind after death to suicide often say, "I just don't understand! We had plans together in the near future." Or "She had everything going for her." As a grief therapist, I hear the question of "WHY?" replayed over and over, sometimes for years. By continuing to learn about the suicidal mind, I can help those left behind attempt to make sense of their loved one's desperation, and suicide. Remember, those who are left behind are simply attempting to find a logical explanation for an illogical act.

What Jenny shares with you throughout *Suicide & Sequins* is her very real encounter of trying to make sense out of something that is nonsensical and finding acceptance that she may never truly understand all of it. Jenny pours her heart out on the pages that follow in order to help the next Survivor behind her. She has shared things with you that are raw and at times challenging for her to share. Jenny has been intentional not to glamourize or dilute her reality. If you've lost someone to suicide the world can feel like one big sham! You may feel like you don't know who or what you can trust. Jenny brings her truth, and she shares important details of her journey. The world is confusing enough without feeling like others are trying to tiptoe around your shattered reality. It's important to note that if some of what you read in these pages are challenging for you, it is absolutely okay to set this book down for some time. Just as grief ebbs and flows, you may also take a break and pick up where you left off when the time feels right to you.

I've read many books on suicide loss in my career, but never one with so much honesty and hope. Jenny recounts, with vulnerability, her reality of what it is like to experience suicide loss, followed by the dedicated work it takes to heal from it, and the life filled with genuine joy and passion on the other side of it. Jenny is the perfect example of how—with time—pain and joy can live cohesively.

Jenny not only shares her story, but she provides you with lists of action items that helped her heal, with the hope that some of those tips will speak to you and can be put into your personal toolbox. She does all this while wearing pink, and while her lips are curved up at either end. This book, *Suicide & Sequins*, is a true gift to the grief and loss community and I am so happy that you have chosen to make it a part of your healing experience.

Jill McMahon, LPC (licensed professional counselor)
Trauma and grief specialist
Private practice owner

Introduction

My oldest childhood memory is of my pet goldfish at age four. While I can't remember his name, I do recall he lived in a round fish bowl amidst some brightly colored rocks with one little fake tropical palm tree. He was a happy goldfish. I watched him swim around until I was in a hypnotic trance.

He lived a simple life. No problems. No fuss. Like rain, food came out of the sky. He needed no plate or a fork. A sunlit room and morning cartoon time with me and my sister provided him with a great life. He was the greatest pet ever. My buddy.

Of course, as a child, I wanted to show my buddy what life was all about. I wanted him to breathe some air just like me. I wanted to pet him, so he would feel loved. I knew he was missing out on so much more, and I was going to show him the life!

It was time to carry out my master plan. I was ready to take him out of that boring bowl of water and pet him. We were going to connect on a whole other level. He was going to be so excited and overwhelmed with glee.

I carefully reached into that fishbowl. I didn't want to hurt him. I wanted it to be a nice ride. But he kept slipping out of my hands until I did a quick swoop up with my hands. How about that! It worked!

He landed on the back of the couch, and onto the floor behind the coffee table. Oh man! I hoped I didn't hurt him! He flopped around on the floor. He was obviously super excited already, and we hadn't even gotten started. I had the biggest Kool-Aid smile as I celebrated in his joy!

I needed to pick him up though because there was so much more I wanted to show him. I still hadn't petted and hugged him. I was trying so hard to reach him. I had my entire body sprawled over the arm of the couch as I reached behind the coffee table. My armpit was rubbing on the side of the coffee table, and it was really starting to hurt as I kept reaching. I would get him, but his wriggling was making it impossible to grasp him. Ugh! I couldn't get a hold on him.

My knees and right shoulder were on the table as I continued to reach with my left arm. I was not even close to getting him. I got down on the floor and tried to reach around the table, but no luck whatsoever. I couldn't even see him to know where to grab. How was I going to get him?!

I got back up on the table and twisted myself like a pretzel again to reach him. Now he wasn't moving. Jeez! This wasn't turning out well at all. This wasn't the experience I had in mind for him. Suddenly, my arm was wet and colorful rocks went everywhere as I knocked the fishbowl over. I remember thinking, *I'm going to get in so much trouble!*

That's the last I remember of that fiasco. I'm sure at some point I learned of his death because the end of my memory leaves me sad, although I didn't yet understand what had really happened. I just thought he was disappointed in being behind a table and not with me. But, of course, he died.

It seems so crazy I can remember something that happened over 40 years ago. But this memory has been ingrained in my mind forever. It was that impactful. It has played out too many times in my adulthood. I had three immediate family members pass before their time under tragic circumstances. They were a lot like the goldfish, while I thought everything was fine. The goldfish represented the beauty of the loved ones I've lost in my life. In my suicide losses, I knew things were rough much like reaching for that goldfish behind the coffee table, and then, BAM! Story over. My loved one was gone. My attempt to save them was futile. Then, the overwhelming guilt of it being my fault.

Isn't that weird how that played out again and again? Know what's weirder? That goldfish event gave me experience, I think, to handle and cope with the more serious events that happened later in my life. At age four, life was already preparing me by planting a little seed.

It took me a long time to be thankful for that goldfish event... and my tragic losses. I'm not thankful for the losses. I'm thankful for the person I am because of them, and what they have allowed me to offer the world. They've literally given me a life purpose. I'd written God off for so long. I was so mad over what He took from me, what He made me endure, what my boys had to experience at such young ages, for not helping my loved ones, for cutting my loved ones' lives short, and, worse, that my niece had to grow up without her mom and never truly knowing how amazing she was. I was done with God; just over it.

In hindsight, I am grateful for the extra years of life to further process my grief, and I can better understand how life really works. I am able to understand that other things caused these events; poor choices, lack of life experience, mental illness, substance abuse, a broken health care system, and more.

I, in turn, have given grace to my sister and my dad. I've given them grace for making poor choices (and I'm not talking about how they died, because I don't think they chose anything). I'd already given them all my emotional and physical time to help them, up until their untimely deaths. I continue to give time by helping others process similar grief and spreading awareness. I've forgiven them for so many things which will be covered in this book. I understand the circumstances that played into their deaths and stopped blaming them. I understand they were only human and doing the best they could do at those times.

But I still miss them and want them back desperately. All of this happened in a span of 12 years. After all those tragedies, I had two horrible separations with two companies I was loyal-to-the-bone with (one led to a nasty lawsuit), and then I made the big jump to start my own company. I'm so proud of myself for where I'm at mentally and spiritually after all the trauma I've endured.

Through my experiences with grief, I hope to help those who are struggling with the impact of suicide. But I also want my readers to know that the experience of grief that I talk about in this book isn't relegated only to suicide. There are many types of grief and people respond to them differently. Grief can manifest from other life events other than losing a loved one. It could come from a divorce, or a breakup, a traumatic lawsuit, the failure of a business, or even bankruptcy. The feelings of grief are a universal human emotion and I hope that this book can offer some hope and light to all of those who are struggling with it.

I now know my life purpose:

To give others hope by vulnerably sharing my story. To help others journey through their grief in productive and healthy ways. To offer a glimmer of light to people when they find themselves in the dark pits of grief. To help people who are grieving and help teach them to give themselves grace and understanding during their journeys.

This book is my gift to the world, so those in need may have insight from someone who is still on her grief journey. Who are you supposed to turn to? Not just anybody gets it. They can't get it; they've never experienced it. My hope is that what I share in this book will give others comfort, insight, tears, understanding, and love. It's excruciatingly hard to write about these things. It's like reliving the events again. I'm peeling off the scab of those wounds. I'm definitely having to process my grief all over on a very personal level, questioning my very existence at times. Some chapters took many attempts to finish, because my eyes were swollen shut from crying over and over. I'm not sure I can read a few of these chapters again. I just want to pack those memories, folded nicely, and stacked on the far, far basement shelf of my mind.

There's no finish line to your grief. You don't "get over it." You don't "move on." You learn to live each day, which gets easier through love and understanding. It takes forced emotional investment and time. But there's hope. I promise. Look at me. I've been through more shit regarding tragic deaths than most people will EVER experience in their lifetime. Believe me, untimely deaths are much harder to process than the natural order of life. But you are not alone, and that's why I'm sharing my story. I see the glimmer of hope in people's eyes as they see me living a positive, joyous life with my sequins on after they hear about my journey. It's like a sense of relief for their own grief. So, I write this book to offer that to a bigger and broader audience.

You can do this.

You will do this.

Your life will be beautiful with a history allowing you to be uniquely magnificent.

Chapter 1

The Unimaginable Call

It's Friday, April 14, 2000, and my cell phone rings while I'm at work. It's an unknown number. I answer, and it's someone who identifies herself as a hospital social worker. If you've ever received a call from a social worker, it's safe to say it's not good news. I realized this while on the phone with her. She said, "We need you to come to the hospital to be there for your sister." These words are forever ingrained in my mind.

"What's wrong?" I asked. She shared there had been an incident with my niece, Gwynnie. I asked myself, *Did she break a leg? Did she burn herself? It must be something serious like that. What the heck is the urgency?* She wouldn't tell me what happened but wanted me to head to the hospital right away to be there for my sister. I was starting to panic so I started cursing at her. I actually called her a "bitch" a few times. She calmly continued to tell me to get to the hospital. She was a real trooper tolerating my unproductive name-calling stunt.

I finally gave up as I realized I could just call my sister. I was frantically calling my sister, literally blowing her phone up. No answer. What the heck?! I was crying out of frustration and confusion. I had no idea what

I was about to learn, but I was anxious, nonetheless. I checked my phone constantly. *Was the ringer on*?

Someone at work insisted they drive me to the hospital. Unbeknownst to me, the hospital requested someone drive me and leave all radios off. The car couldn't move fast enough. My coworker driving me was a safe, slow driver like my dad, so I was about to become unglued. I was shouting in my head, *Come on! Put the pedal to the metal! Was my ringer on?* Why wasn't my sister calling me? I texted her too. Texting was no easy task because we used qwerty at the time. I sent my text in all caps thinking she would finally call me as if the 100+ phone calls didn't give it away already.

I kept wondering, *Is my ringer on? How am I going to get back to work to get my car?* Mind you, this was pre-Uber times. I lived in Tucson and was commuting to Phoenix three days per week. *Did I leave my work computer on?* I don't remember how, but I organized someone to pick up my kids from daycare in Tucson. I called my husband, Chuck Gibson, and told him I was on my way to the hospital for Jacque. I was bitching because they made this seem really serious, but they were not telling me anything. He was heading there too. *Was my ringer on?* I couldn't focus. My mind kept jumping from one thought to another, making me disoriented and sick to my stomach. What. The. F;ck?!

We pulled up to the hospital and there were news vans everywhere like a swarm of bees. We could barely find our way to the emergency entrance. I was pissed because the crowd was holding me back and I needed to get to Jacque.

As I walked in the hospital, I was immediately approached and asked if I was Jenny Gibson. I was then escorted to a nearby door. I thought it was odd that they knew who I was. It took so long to walk that 100 or so feet to the door. It felt like the old cartoons where they run down an endless hall full of doors, passing them on both sides. I wanted to run.

All was quiet and confusing. I still didn't understand what the big, damn deal was. I mean, it couldn't be that big of a deal if Jacque didn't answer my call, right? She surely would have called me. I didn't yet know what I was about to find out, because we weren't able to reach each other by design of the hospital staff. As I opened that door, I did it casually as if being so close to seeing Jacque lessened the urgency. Then, I saw her:

On the floor.

Curled into the fetal position on her side.

With her head cradled in between her arms as if to protect her ears from hearing anymore.

Crying in a tone that shook my soul.

Begging, "Nooooooo, not my baby!"

I knew.

I fell to my knees and wrapped myself around her in an all-encompassing hold.

It turned out my niece, Gwynnie, was the first drowning victim of the Arizona summer. It was all over the radio and TV already. *"First drowning of the summer."* For the news station, it was like a badge of honor to capture this story to get more ratings.

There was no way to describe to someone the pain of losing an innocent child. And weren't your children always innocent in death anyhow? I literally couldn't put this kind of loss in words. My current husband told me once about when first responders reset his heart. He said it felt so horrible, like his heart fell down and his chest went empty. His whole body gave out.

When he told that story, it always brought me back to the moment I found out we lost Gwynnie. My heart was gone. It was like an anxiety attack. My heart raced so fast that it suddenly didn't feel like it was there anymore. Like anxiety to infinity.

As I walked into that room, the air was thick. It was almost a tangible item I could touch as if a ball of pressure was caving in around me. I listened to my sister pleading desperately to have this be a dream. "Why?! Why did He take her?" she cried. She then pleaded, "Please, let this be a dream! Please!!! I'll do anything!" I kept thinking, *We are in a dream, right? How in the hell can this be real?* The pain was something awful. How could that be real? This didn't happen to you. It happened to other people, and you read about it and moved on. I thought losing a limb and bleeding out would feel better than this. If you asked me to choose, I'd choose the limb option without hesitation and with a sigh of relief.

Fast forward because I literally couldn't remember what happened next. It was like my brain said, *Whoa! Hold up! We need to unload data to process this nonsense.* So, it threw my memories into an incinerator. Here I am 20 years later, and I still have no memory of what happened, even after having time to process my grief. It was like the grief was so big and heavy, that there was no room for long-term storage. Just burn it. I still can't figure out why my brain didn't burn that event instead. I think remembering what happened would be much better even though it's hard.

The next thing I remember was being asked if we wanted to see Gwynnie. *Holy cow! Jacque's prayers were answered! They saved her!* I thought Jacque felt the same because I saw the quick glimmer of hope in her eyes. Shortly thereafter, the look of doom returned once they explained, "It's just her body. She looks like she's sleeping." They would only let Gwynnie's parents, my brother-in-law Jeff, and sister Jacque go in. I wasn't so much disappointed I couldn't see her, but that I was being separated from my sister in this time of desperate need.

I took this time to call my mom. She knew something was up, but not yet what it was. I don't remember much about this call. I just remember she was flying out within six hours. I called my dad after that. My dad was at Lake Roosevelt with his friends. I felt so bad calling him, but he would've been mad had I not called him. I was actually surprised he had cell phone service. I tried to pull the whole social-worker-routine and not tell him. I was afraid of him driving from the lake all the way back to town with that information. The heartache while driving alone would be debilitating. Funny, he asked the same question that I initially did. "Did she break a leg?" It's as if the biggest extremity of your body is the most severe injury there could be, therefore an emergency. When you have a baby, the thought of death never even occurs to you. Somehow, he got it out of me.

Next thing I knew, the phone was silent. I called him back. No answer. I called him again. No answer. Then he called me. He told me he was heading home, and he was crying like a baby. I begged him to drive home with a friend. He told me he would, but he didn't. I later found out that when I told him she died, he threw his phone, and had to go find it. That was the delay in calling me back.

Then, a nurse came out and asked me if I wanted to see Gwynnie. As I walked into the bright white room, I saw my sister and Jeff leaning over Gwynnie in excruciating pain. Pain you could almost put color to. The pain was black and cold, and quickly blinded you from the bright white, sterile room. White was the color of an angel, which was ironically drowned out by the black of pain. It was so eerie. Gwynnie looked like you could just wake her up. She was a precious, sleeping baby. At least, that was what my dream was telling me. Seeing her brought this odd sense of relief, like she really wasn't gone. She was right there. Your mind does mysterious things to protect its health.

The look on Jeff and Jacque's faces as they tried to process this pain a human wasn't designed for was killing me.

You see, I, more or less, raised Jacque and my brother, Johnny, (2.5 years and 5.5 years younger than me respectively) with my dad, so there was this unusual dynamic of me being both the oldest sister and a mother figure to them. We were raised in a single parent home with our dad in Phoenix, Arizona. Oftentimes, he worked nights or odd hours, requiring my help to take care of all of us in his absence. Our mom relocated to Colorado when I was eleven. I started cooking, doing laundry, and helping as a mother in the home when I was just eleven. I helped my siblings get ready and get to school in the mornings. I helped them with homework, homework timeliness, and signing off on their homework. I took on a lot of parental responsibilities when I was young. To this day, my brother considers me both his sister and his mom. As a mother figure and the oldest sister, I felt this awful pressure to make this pain go away for Jacque. I wanted to absorb the pain, even if it ultimately meant giving my life for Gwynnie. But it was not within my control. I was at the mercy of this tragedy.

Gwynnie had a white sheet draped over most of her body. It looked like Jeff and Jacque pulled it down a bit to see more of their precious baby girl, their only child. Jeff allowed me to sit in his place. I brushed Gwynnie's face as if to wake her. She was cold. No response. Not even an eye flutter. I swear to you I thought this was a dream. I had no doubt. I spent months after this waking up every day crying because it was real.

A human being should not have to go through this. It causes brain trauma. Your brain is literally injured, and only a spin of the wheel will show what the turn out will be. Think about it. Your brain is processing your thoughts, so wouldn't these overwhelming thoughts kill brain cells or, at least, break the circuits of information? It must cause inflammation in the brain. Wouldn't it affect the very essence of your soul? I don't know how counselors do it. They have to listen to these tragic, God-awful stories all the time. Does their brain get injured? Perhaps eventually they become jaded, like most HR personnel who have brain trauma caused by empathy overload. The same could be said of many professions, such as first responders, social workers, or attorneys.

I continued to caress Gwynnie with my hands and give her kisses. I didn't want to leave her but knew I would have to soon. It was like a merciful goodbye because we had to do this while she had already passed. It was okay, though, because there was not much of the day left, and tomorrow I would wake up from this dream to the start of a great weekend.

****

Gwyneth Winter Mitchell
February 1999 - April 2000
Age 14 months

Chapter 2

Wishing It Was a Dream

I woke up groggy, almost like a still-drunk hangover, with a severe burning sensation in my eyes. They were so swollen that it was difficult to get them open 100%. I thought, *Wait! This is real?!?! This was supposed to be a bad dream.* I immediately realized it wasn't and started bawling. I sat up while doubled over the side of my bed wailing. I felt like my heart had fallen to the darkest pits of my belly, and I was empty behind my rib cage. I bawled for at least ten minutes. I kept asking, "How can this pain be real?! How can God put me through this pain?" Throughout my life, He came to mind in my times of despair. I was quick to blame Him when things were bad, but I didn't trust Him with all things. We'll get back to that later.

Oh my gosh! What about Jeff and Jacque? If I'm feeling this, I can't even imagine what they are feeling. I'm barely able to comprehend my own pain, I thought. I called Jacque. There was no answer. I thought she was probably sleeping, so I got ready and headed over.

I didn't brush my teeth. I didn't shower. I was barely able to dress myself, and the whole time I just kept weeping out loud. I'd calm myself only to later have quick "this is real" moments, which made me burst into tears. It was a non-stop cycle. My eyes were always swollen and burning, my shoulders always slumped over, my head always down. The pain was literally pulling my entire being down from my body to my soul; everything just falling into a dark pit. I kept wondering where my heart was. It literally felt like my heart was missing from my chest. I couldn't understand how it was still beating. I just wanted to wither away and leave this pain. It was so awful.

Driving was a whole other task. Driving should be illegal in the first week of grief. I swore it was worse than texting and driving. I could barely see the road through water-filled eyes. I struggled to even keep my head up to watch the road. My head kept wanting to leave this world and wallow in my tears. Somehow or other, I got there. I walked inside, and there was Jacque. These were the words that came to mind as I saw her:

Sitting and staring straight ahead
Eyes not moving; like doll eyes with nothing in them
Red and swollen
Emotionless
Unattached to this reality
Comatose

I got to her and gave her a huge hug and started bawling. She came out of her escape from reality and started asking me, "Why?" over and over while she cried. Actually, it was more like "Whyyyyyyyyyy?" She begged me to make this stop and be a bad dream.

I could only imagine how waking up was for her. Her morning routine of getting Gwynnie ready was not needed. I was sure she went to Gwynnie's room to make sure this wasn't real only to be shaken to her soul again. To this day, I wonder how many mornings she continued to do that. The soulful pain in her cries tore me up. Each cry was like a jagged knife through my chest—my empty chest. I felt like we were spinning in one of those carnival rides that makes you sick. You know the one. You are inside, up against a wall, and you start to slide up the wall as it spins. Like that. You are standing still but spinning. Everything is flashing in front of your eyes, but you can't quite make anything out. The feeling of needing to vomit overwhelms you, but grief is a raw emotion you can't remedy by getting off the ride. This is a non-stop ride. Non-stop, spinning out of control all the while trying to maintain a sense of being.

I was supposed to help my sister as her oldest sister and mother figure, but it seemed I couldn't help in any meaningful way. In hindsight, I know I helped her, but, at the time, it didn't seem meaningful unless I brought Gwynnie back. So, on top of everything else, I was beating myself up over the guilt of not delivering on my familial duties. I started to feel inadequate. I felt like God chose the wrong person to be by her side. How in the heck could I possibly be equipped to help? They didn't teach you this stuff in school. They didn't teach you coping skills in school. This was a wake-up call in which you realized you were never prepared for this. And can you ever *really* be prepared for this? If life said to you, "One day your soul is going to be ripped to shreds and trampled on, and you must go on." What do you do to prepare for that? If you've never been in the storm, can you really ever be ready? It doesn't matter, I suppose, because life didn't give us a heads up.

Each day, I woke up certain this dream would be over. I say "day" because I slept through most mornings, so I only had to get through half of the day. And every damn day, I learned it wasn't a dream and wept. Every. Damn. Day. Sometimes I cried out loud. Sometimes I wept in silence, literally wallowing in my own self-pity. I kept repeating, "This is a dream." A dream—a nightmare—come true.

I now have a whole newfound compassion for others in these types of griefs. A grief reality that now makes you feel bad, because you didn't understand people who were grieving before. People just hear of it and move on, but when you're in the wake of it, you don't get to move on. You must stay, processing it while everyone else goes about life as it was before, but it's never the same for those in grief, who feel seemingly left behind. You begin to wonder why people are not asking how you are or stop reaching out after a few months of time goes by. They think you've moved on too, or it seems that way. They stop talking about it with you, but you are always thinking about it.

It would be nice if people would call and ask if they can help with anything. Or simply say I am bringing over some food. Or "I was thinking about you today. I wanted to check in. Want to talk about anything? You can cry on my shoulder." Or maybe "What are you doing today?" Or "How are you handling going to work?" Don't ask "How are you doing?" or "How are you feeling?" because the answer is pretty much always the same: horrible, shitty, etc. We might say "okay," but we are lying to make you feel better versus how we really feel.

Nobody wanted to talk about Gwynnie anymore for fear they might upset us. We *WANTED* to talk about her. Sure, we would get upset, but not at the person that asked about her. We were forever grateful somebody brought up her name. We *wanted* her memory to stay alive. We would have thought many things and maybe shared them and thanked them for talking about her! Please understand our tears, and the peace you give us all for remembering her. They're happy-sad tears. We're happy she's both not forgotten, and someone is mentioning her. We are sad as we lost her before her time, and now we have all this love we can no longer give.

That's what grief ultimately is—the love you cannot give anymore. You have to figure out what to do with all this overflowing love. Your recipient isn't there to take it off your hands with their smiles, kisses, and hugs, with their mere presence. You walk and leave a trail of love behind you like pooled blood from your broken heart.

My sister was battling overwhelming guilt. We never once spoke of it, but I knew it was there. I feel bad to this day. I always gave her flack for not getting counseling for her grief. In hindsight, I could have just brought it up and talked about it with her myself. Maybe that would have helped. Interestingly, I couldn't even bring up the topic of Gwynnie with my sister, something I suggested others do.

Gwynnie drowned at the babysitter's house. The babysitter was a great woman who had been watching Gwynnie since she was three weeks old. I went with my sister to interview her while Jacque was pregnant with Gwynnie. She was a perfect fit. I still stand by that selection.

The day Gwynnie drowned, the babysitter had laid Gwynnie down for a nap like she'd done every day. While she was napping, I believe the babysitter was folding laundry in her room and may have been on the phone. She had five older kids; I think the oldest was fifteen. Her kids were swimming in their backyard pool. When they were done swimming, someone left the door open. Gwynnie got up from her nap unusually and, unbeknownst to the babysitter, she went outside to the pool.

The babysitter was a mess from the loss of Gwynnie. To this day, I continue to get so worked up when people comment on Facebook about child drownings, or a child left in a car with horrible judgment. You can practically feel some of them spitting on the responsible parties. Me? Even from day one, I always empathized with the babysitter. This was a tragic accident. It couldn't have been more tragic if you ask me. But it *WAS* an accident. We have accidents every day. We misplace our keys, we spill a drink, we trip, we forget something, we get into car accidents. Sometimes we aren't there when we are needed most. Needless to say, some accidents have dire consequences—life changing consequences.

There was chatter amongst our family that the babysitter had better not be at the funeral. I sat with Jacque and explained to her that she loved Gwynnie. She genuinely loved Gwynnie like she was her own daughter, and not letting her attend the funeral wasn't right. We didn't need to uninvite her to let her know we were disappointed in what happened. She certainly was already beating herself up worse than any of us could. She was a human being that was suffering, and she deserved to say goodbye to Gwynnie as well. Jacque obliged and allowed it. Only a select few even knew she would be there. We just asked that she not say who she was, but you knew at the funeral. She was in the back of the church, a sobbing mess. She could barely walk and had someone helping her in and out of the church.

I went to pick up Gwynnie's clothes, shoes, and the 911-call tape from the police station. I still have her clothes and her shoes she was wearing. I still have that tape. I'll never listen to it again. The love and panic combined in the babysitter's voice as she screamed for Gwynnie to wake up while giving CPR is something I never need to hear again. Ever. I shouldn't call it screaming. It was more of a high-pitched shrill of sheer panic that freezes you to your core. I just got goosebumps and tears in my eyes typing these words. I listened to it once and I put it away forever. I knew then that she genuinely loved Gwynnie. It was an accident you can never explain or recover 100% from. She certainly would be scarred for life, because, technically, she was at fault with Gwynnie in her care. I felt it was the right thing to do to let her attend the funeral, and I'm so glad we allowed her to.

My Sister's Guilt Was Heavy

A few months prior to Gwynnie drowning, my sister, Jacque, told me that the babysitter had moved to a new home with a pool without a fence. Jacque felt uncomfortable about it and asked her to put in a fence. I don't know what ever became of those conversations, but they were ultimately too late in resolution. A lesson hard learned. And that was where my sister's guilt was sure to have come from. She knew about the pool and didn't take the necessary steps to avoid what happened. But, in hindsight, who thinks that would happen to them?! Hindsight is always 20/20.

In the eight years following the loss of Gwynnie, I never once talked to my sister about her guilt. Ironically, today, I still feel guilty about it. I wonder now if not talking about it made her feel even more guilty. It's like we all knew but didn't talk about it. Perhaps it was like this white elephant at every gathering for her. I feel so bad about that now. Kind of like how I mentioned no one talking about Gwynnie prior, I did that to my sister without even knowing it was damaging.

The detective told me he thought Gwynnie was in the pool for about five minutes. They briefly got a faint heartbeat from her but could not maintain it. She missed surviving the drowning by mere minutes.

I urge everyone to teach your children to swim when they are just weeks old. They can be taught to float with their mouths up, allowing them to breathe and it gives you time to find them. As children get more capable and coordinated, instructors teach them how to get to steps and out of the pool. But learning to float is crucial, and infants can learn that skill. Don't underestimate them. I didn't know this information then. I wish I had because that's the advice I would have given Jacque. I just wasn't equipped with this information at twenty-five years old even though I had two boys, ages four and two, at the time. If Gwynnie had swim lessons, she would have been found floating face up and breathing. Sometimes, I imagine what life would be like for our family with just that one *little* tweak. It's so beautiful to visualize, but it's a destiny that will never become a reality.

A few months after Gwynnie passed, my sister shared with me that her brother-in-law, Daniel, had told her to watch Gwynnie around pools. This was just four months prior to Gwynnie's drowning. Daniel was schizophrenic, so she blew it off as crazy talk. That is the problem with the general public's understanding of mental illness. We so quickly dehumanized someone with a mental condition as if they couldn't possibly know what they were talking about or have insight of any kind. We call them crazy to explain it away. They lose their humanity in many uneducated people's eyes.

Daniel was a total brainiac student at Arizona State University. One day, he just wasn't the same anymore and needed care to live his life. I've heard stories of people developing mental conditions that seem to have been brought on by smoking marijuana for the first time or trying other substances, hell sometimes there's no plausible reason at all. I still curiously wonder how and why he suddenly changed. Sadly, he passed away from a choking accident in 2017, so now I'll never be able to ask him. His brain just changed. Perhaps, his condition also gave him some sort of psychic ability everyone was unaware of. Jacque said his comment was made at a family Christmas gathering. He got uncomfortably close to her face and looked her straight in the eyes to say, "Watch Gwynnie around pools." It was a shame she didn't take that as a sign, considering the babysitter's recent move that worried her. I don't think she even pieced any of that together until after the fact.

Gwynnie's wake and funeral were so beautiful. She looked so angelic. She was in a beautiful pink dress Jeff and Jacque shopped forever for. Can you imagine having to go out in public to shop for the final outfit your daughter will ever wear? It just broke my heart. Imagine selecting a funeral home, casket, plot, service, etc. for your baby? It was so unnatural. You had to approach it like a robot—just getting it done.

Hours and hours were spent collecting and scanning photos, and then creating a slideshow for the funeral. This was before the technology we have now. You literally had to scan each photo, edit, and save them. But everyone pulled together considering this tragedy to put together a beautiful, memorable service for Gwynnie.

Funerals are weird. You want to say hi to people you haven't seen in so long, but you are so out of it. I don't even remember who came and who didn't come. I can still see the crowd of people though and the line of cars to the gravesite. Seeing all that love and support was beautiful and heart-touching.

We all handle these types of events differently. At one point, I hid in a bathroom stall to have a complete breakdown. My dad's nose started bleeding badly as he tried to hold his tears while viewing Gwynnie in her casket at the wake. Blood was all over his shirt. I was crushed seeing my dad so torn up by this. Dad never cried. And he was sobbing but still trying to hold it in. So much so that it caused the nosebleed. I don't remember much of anything else. It was such a blur. I just remember Gwynnie looked beautiful. She would always be beautiful.

My last memory of Gwynnie alive will be forever treasured. My mom, Jacque, and Gwyneth drove from Phoenix to visit us in Tucson. One of my favorite pictures was taken on that trip. It's the only one I have with me, my sister, and our kids together. Gwynnie needed a nap. She wasn't familiar with the house so she wouldn't lay down. I laid down with her. She was so calm and felt cared for enough to slumber. At that moment, it felt wonderful to be her aunt. To this day, I can close my eyes and feel her breathing on my chest as she slept. It's a precious moment I'm forever grateful for.

Chapter 3

The Complexity of Grief

My sister, Jacque, was an amazing human being. She was a blast to hang with, funny, caring, supportive, and, like any Clifton (that's our family name), she would give you the shirt off her back. She was someone to admire and look up to. I wish she continued to know that about herself after losing Gwynnie, but she seemed to let guilt and grief define her worth. I don't believe my sister ever got appropriate therapy for her grief. She had a psychiatrist, but they only medicated her. I wish I knew then what I know now about health; it's not just working out and eating. It's about positive mental health which includes:

- mindfulness and meditation
- self-love and acceptance
- self-forgiveness
- self-care
- self-awareness
- self-empathy

True Health is an Inside Job

True health is taking care of yourself including your self-talk. It's treating yourself how you want others to treat you, basically the golden rule. I know Jacque struggled to identify with any of that after Gwynnie. Hell, she probably struggled with most of that even before Gwynnie. I don't think many of us know how or do half of that by the time we are thirty. And yet she lost Gwynnie when she was twenty-two.

Imagine being just twenty-two years old and grieving the loss of your only child. Here I was trying to live my own life by the minute, or hours, each day. I couldn't even imagine her grief. We all grieve so differently. I just wish I would have been more instrumental in helping her grieve. Again, I wish I knew then what I know now.

I woke up nearly every day for months weeping. That was no exaggeration, every day. I still, twenty years later, wake up on rare occasions, shocked that this is real and cry. If I was feeling that I couldn't possibly imagine what Jeff and Jacque were feeling. So, who am I to judge?

Can Baby Lauren Take Away Some of That Pain?

My sister had her second daughter, Lauren, twenty months after losing Gwynnie. Lauren is a beautiful human being, and I am so glad my sister was able to be an active mom again. Raising Lauren brought Jacque so much joy. My sister was always one of those kids growing up that aspired to be a mom, so Lauren gave her life again. She lit a fire within my sister. Jacque was Jacque again. It was so wonderful, and I felt so much relief for her. We were turning a corner!

That was why I didn't think much of Jacque drinking alcohol. I thought for sure it would stop now that Lauren was here. That's the thing though;

Lauren was not brought onto the earth for my sister to bandage her grief. Jacque loved Lauren for the child she was. She wasn't a replacement for Gwynnie. Lauren was child number two, Jacque's youngest daughter. I knew that, but I thought it would help her overcome the grief of losing Gwynnie. It didn't. She still needed to deal with that grief.

She still missed Gwynnie, and she still felt guilty that her life was cut so soon. Nothing was going to make that go away except therapy. She was on antidepressants and bipolar disorder medications, but those didn't make it go away either. You need to process your grief verbally and actively. You can't cover it, shun it, ignore it, etc. Well, you can try, but it will always be there in a festering way. You can deal with your stuff, or it'll deal with you.

To top all of this off, Jeff and Jacque separated and divorced shortly thereafter. The stress of losing a daughter and Jacque's increasing addiction were too much for them, I imagine. Amongst the most stressful things in life are death, bankruptcy, divorce, and moving. She was grieving the death of Gwynnie, and then divorcing and moving out of their house. That was a lot of stuff. So, what did she do? She drank it all away. All these circumstances drove her drinking to an all-time high.

Alcoholism and Holding Secrets

Jacque continued to self-medicate, but it only made the pain worse. I didn't quite understand it. I still don't understand it, but I know alcoholism is ugly. I am a twelve-year clean smoker after twenty years of smoking cigarettes. In my experience watching Jacque, it seemed drinking may be a harder habit to break than smoking. And, damn, quitting smoking was so hard. Alcohol really takes hold of a person. At the time, I just let it be. I thought, *Who am I to judge?* In the meantime, things got really ugly.

I didn't tell my family that Jacque was drinking. I hid it from them. Most of our family was in Colorado at the time. Jacque hid her drinking from my brother and Dad, who still lived in Phoenix, so they weren't really concerned about her. I was certain my dad didn't even know at all. He was raised by an alcoholic father who was abusive towards his mom and two younger brothers. His dad was running around town with another woman as his mother was dying in the hospital from leukemia. His mom died when he was nineteen, and he was always very anti-drinking after that. In fact, he despised alcoholics. I had been told my dad would have a beer every now and then, but I only recall seeing him drink one time in my life. I remember it so vividly, it rarely ever happened. I was shocked when I saw him drinking that beer. Whether he drank or not, he did a damn good job of keeping his kids away from it. I didn't grow up thinking I needed to drink to have a good time. As a result, I was often the designated driver. Today, if I know I'll be drinking any alcohol, I organize a ride or use Uber or Lyft.

Jacque came to live with me when I was a single mom. It was just me and my sons, so it was easy enough to have her live there as well. I don't remember why she had to move in with me, but by that time she had been drinking heavily for three years. That was when I learned how bad her drinking was. Many nights when I came home, she was slurring her speech badly. After a few months, she started smelling like tequila all the time. She acted so strangely about her tequila bottles. She didn't throw them away as she drank them. Instead, she accumulated them in her closet and then threw them away in bulk later. When I went into her room, I'd encounter a stockpile of empty bottles. At other times, I'd find the kitchen trash can filled to the top with tequila bottles. She wouldn't even bother to hide it from me. Perhaps, that was why I didn't hassle her about it. Could it be that bad if she wasn't hiding it?

There'd always be an open bottle of tequila in the kitchen. My sons started asking me if Jacque was drinking. I asked her to please not drink in front of the kids anymore and to stay in her room if she was going to be slurring. She willingly agreed but it continued. I spoke to her about her daughter, Lauren, witnessing this all the time. When I asked if she was drinking and driving too, she said, "No." I reminded her that this type of environment wasn't good for Lauren.

After nothing changed, I asked her if she could find an apartment to live in on her own. She agreed quickly. It seemed she was tired of feeling monitored and wanted some privacy. So, when she moved out, it was more or less amicable with no hard feelings.

A few weeks after she moved out, my dad was at my house. He casually asked, "Why did you kick Jacque out?" His tone indicated he was clearly upset. I asked, "Why did you say I kicked her out?" He let me know that was what Jacque told him. I don't even remember what I told him, but I didn't tell him about the drinking. I did it more to protect him than Jacque though. He was so anti-drinking that I didn't want him to learn that about her and be upset. This was about 3.5 years after we lost Gwynnie. Wasn't that enough? In retrospect, I should have said something because the road after that was rough. I could have used his help or advice. Maybe we would have been able to help her sooner.

Although Jacque had a great job, a beautiful downtown apartment, a car many envied on the road, and a wonderful daughter, the grief and guilt always were lurking in the background. At one point, Lauren's daycare called me after they closed asking if I knew where Jacque was. I tried calling Jacque repeatedly, but nothing. When I went to pick up Lauren, I decided to take her to my home and then go back downtown to Jacque's apartment. I didn't want Lauren seeing whatever I was going to see when I arrived.

I banged on her door and there was no response. I was frightened. I was afraid she was dead. I kept banging and calling her phone. Finally, I saw something move in the sliver between the barely swaying blinds. Jacque opened the door. She was so drunk. She had drunk herself to an oblivious slumber. She told me she was sick and had to take Nyquil, but she reeked of tequila. I was livid. At this point, I was still the only person in the family that knew the extent of this problem.

The next day I convinced my sister to go to a hospital. She went for three days in lockdown in an inpatient treatment. Apparently, insurance felt a two-night stay wasn't enough time for her to get help, but three nights was. They sent her home to reach out for further help on quitting drinking after three nights. I was so upset. It wasn't long enough for her. How was she going to be better in three nights?

At this point, I told my dad. He asked me why I never told him. I told him I didn't want to hurt him or cause him to be stressed about it. I had such respect for him. He'd fought to keep and raise three kids under the age of six alone. Despite working crazy shifts, he always took care of our household needs. I didn't want to bestow this on him. He told me he was sorry for judging me when I "kicked Jacque out." He finally understood.

Then I shared with my mom and siblings what was happening. Chuck knew, as did his family, who I was able to confide in and seek advice. I wouldn't say my family was shocked to learn of Jacque's drinking, but they were surprised.

By inpatient treatment, Jacque was locked in the facility. She could not leave. Believe me, she didn't want to be there. She wanted to leave so bad for so many reasons, one of which was wanting to drink. Staff escorted visitors through a door. You had to be a visitor on the list and scheduled, otherwise you weren't coming in. I felt bad putting her in a facility like that, but it was the only way she was going to get any help.

Her drinking was so bad that she had visible shakes you could see from ten feet away, even in her face. She was so embarrassed to be seen that way even by her own sister. How long did she stay sober after leaving inpatient treatment? It wasn't long at all. I knew it right away because she immediately stopped shaking. She told me later she tried only having a few shots of tequila to get rid of the shakes while at work, but those shots quickly increased and became out of control. Could I blame her? Imagine going to work visibly shaking. What would you tell your co-workers? You were in your 20s and seemed healthy. Of course, most of the office knew she had a drinking problem by now due to her absence and how she smelled of alcohol.

Months later, after she attempted suicide by sitting in her car with it running while in her garage, she went for a five-night stay at the same in-patient facility. I don't remember how many months later this was after the first stay, but it was only a few months afterward. She really didn't want to go into in-patient care, because she didn't want her work to know. She was an amazing accountant at a big law firm. She was a true functioning alcoholic.

It's a sad thing, in-patient care. When you need it, it's not private. Where are you supposed to say you were while also using your family medical leave benefits? She had to use that, so she didn't lose her job. So, of course, she had to tell them.

By "them," I mean HR. Let's be real though, HR staff are some of the biggest gossipers I've met in my career. Hell, I'd rather tell the stranger across the way than HR about my problems. It's embarrassing when work knows your business. They find out no matter what. You-know-who in HR tells you-know-what confidentially. Then you-know-what tells you-know-how confidentially. Then you-know-how tells you-know-where confidentially. Before you know it, it gets back to you-know-who in HR, and they are sweatin' bullets that everyone knows. It's true. So, you have this dynamic hindrance to navigate when you're trying to help yourself escape this horrible addiction.

It's interesting though because you fear being judged but mostly everyone understands. Sure, there's probably the few talking smack, but most totally understand how hard life can be. And those few who gossip probably have their own issues they are hiding in the smack talking. Some of them may even have the same problem or someone in their home does, so they can empathize with the situation. But it's still not their business. Time off makes it their business though. So much for HIPAA[1] laws in office/insurance politics. Now I understand why many people don't seek in-patient care. It was the ONLY thing besides organizing care for Lauren that my sister was afraid of.

During both of my in-patient visits with my sister, I brought her cigarettes. I would take pictures of Lauren on my phone, who was three at the time, and show them to her. My sister was so sad when she was in the hospital. It broke my heart. I could literally feel the pain radiating from her while sitting next to her. I could also see the agony in her beautiful, big, blue eyes. She had natural eyelashes women pay good money for. If you wanted to imagine what her eyes looked like, just look at her daughter, Lauren. Genetic replicas.

Jacque made a valiant attempt to mask the pain, but in the end, the pain was visible. You could almost paint it. It was thick in the air like wading in water. I would get her to laugh, and we'd have a great conversation as I intended. But afterward, her eyes returned to the inescapable pain in her heart. I could sense she was disappointed in her life. I would leave with my shoulders hunched over and eyes looking down while racking my brain on what else I could have done. I just wanted to stay there with her until it was gone. Ultimately, I felt like a failure. I was letting her down as a mother figure and a sister. In my perception, I kept disappointing her. I couldn't be there to stop her sadness, suicide attempts, and drinking. I felt like I was just letting her wither away in sadness.

---

[1] https://www.hhs.gov/hipaa/for-professionals/privacy/index.html

At least, those were my thoughts. I'm getting a bit ahead of myself in this book, because I didn't think this at that exact time in my life. But if you really think about it, I most certainly bought us time and lots of it.

A little backstory: Jacque moved from Arizona to live with my mom in Denver during her senior year in high school. She wasn't doing well in school and wanted a fresh start. That new start panned out, and she graduated. She moved back to Phoenix shortly after graduation though. I don't know why she moved back. I don't think I ever asked because I was so excited to have her back. She initially was my roommate. We lived in a tiny one-bedroom apartment. It was heaven. We would have card game nights, just her and me. We would play "War" and listen to our two favorite Patsy Cline cassette tapes nonstop. I have such fond memories of those times.

This was when my sister had her first suicide attempt at age eighteen. I wasn't home when it happened. I don't even know why it happened. I was so shocked. She had taken a shit ton of pills while I wasn't home. While in the hospital, she hallucinated so badly that she asked me to put my seatbelt on as I sat in a chair next to her hospital bed. She proceeded to perform the standard-transmission driving motions with her hands and feet. The doctors said it was hopeful she would come out of it, but there was a slim possibility that it was long-term or permanent. I was so scared for her. I had no idea there were problems.

I then started having my own suicidal thoughts. Suicide ideation happened a lot for me. I didn't have those thoughts before. I think perhaps it plants a seed. But what I've learned since then is that suicide ideation doesn't mean you will act or plan suicide. Many people have suicide ideation, more than you would think. That's not to say we take suicide ideation lightly. It's so complicated.

How many other attempts were there of which I didn't know? Did I save her through a phone call once prior to an attempt? Did I make plans with her to go somewhere together, giving her hope? Did she ever keep her promise she made to me to not do it? I bet the answer was YES to those last three questions. Please keep that in your heart as you continue reading. Know that the work you do may not seem fruitful because of the challenges still in the way, but they are still here with you. They still have a chance to get to a hopeful place. There's still time to do more work. Don't throw your hands up because it's still not good. We most certainly save their lives every time we help. There's no doubt in my mind.

Jacque carried a sadness of disappointment in herself over the loss of Gwynnie. She felt like she couldn't keep it together for her daughter. What mother lets her future children down after the first one dies? I told Jacque this had nothing to do with being a mom. I assured her she was an awesome mom. Lauren was three years old at the time and missed her, she genuinely wanted to go home to her. Lauren wasn't acting like an abused or abandoned child that had been rescued. She was honestly concerned and asking where her mom was. Jacque was good to her and loved her with everything she had. I reminded Jacque so often that she needed help to cope with the loss of Gwynnie. She couldn't love herself until she addressed that. And she couldn't be there for anyone 100% until she loved herself.

Suicide ideation is defined as thinking about, considering, or planning suicide. It's not a psychiatric diagnosis but defines a symptom in the treatment of mental disorders. The risk assessment of suicidal ideation ranges from momentary thoughts to specific planning and preparation. Most people who have suicidal thoughts do not follow through on suicide attempts, but suicidal ideation is considered a risk factor. This symptom is seen with depression and other mood disorders; however, it can involve multiple mental disorders, life events, and family events, all of which may increase the risk of suicidal ideation. If you or someone you know has experienced this, seek out professional medical help to explore your options for treatment.

I've yet to meet anyone that said she talked about Gwynnie with them. Sure, she would talk about losing her first daughter but only vaguely so they could know the source of her woes. She just did not want to face that guilt she carried, but she was facing it every day with alcohol. It was a vicious circle that I believe therapy could have saved her from. I have no clue if she spoke to the therapists in the in-patient care program about Gwynnie in detail, but I know she didn't continue treatment at all or she did briefly upon getting out. She just went back to the alcohol. I still don't get it and never will.

Chapter 4

Turn of the Tide

Months after Jacque's second in-patient treatment, she called me at work. She was slurring her words badly. She was drunk. It was unusual for her to call me like that because she always attempted to hide being drunk. I don't even recall why she called me. I just remember thinking she was a suicide risk. She never said anything that should have made me suspect that, but I felt it in my gut. In retrospect, I'm certain I saved her life that day.

When I asked her if she had been drinking, she responded with the usual "no." I asked where Lauren was, and she said she was at daycare. I asked her why she wasn't at work, and she replied that she wasn't feeling well. I assumed she took Lauren to daycare and came home to drink. I hung up the phone and immediately called Chuck, my ex-husband. I asked him to meet me at Jacque's place to get Lauren's car seat so we could pick her up from daycare.

I arrived at the apartment before Chuck. Jacque was surprised to see me. I told her I was there to take her to alcohol/drug treatment. I had a bad feeling about Jacque and needed to trust my gut instinct. She said she was fine and got pissy and claimed I was overreacting. She refused to go. I told her I would call 911 and tell them she was threatening suicide. She said, nearly spitting in anger, "That's a lie." I let her know I could easily live with that lie but felt something was up.

Let's stop there. If you are reading this book, you know where this story eventually leads. There are moments in life when you get these weird feelings. LISTEN TO THEM. Your intuition is powerful. Give yourself credit. You don't always need proof or a concrete reason for what you do. Sorry, not sorry, to those who disagree. I wasn't always that fortunate in listening to my intuition about the end of this journey.

I suggested she pack a bag. She refused. I told her, "If you don't pack your bag, you're not going to have everything you want and I'm not bringing it." I also bribed her with a carton of cigarettes, and explained that if she didn't go with me, she wasn't going to get her cigarettes. As a result, she'd have to suffer without both her smokes and alcohol. The thought of both was unbearable. Thus, she started packing fast.

She was throwing stuff around and into her suitcase when Chuck arrived to get Lauren's car seat. She was throwing a tantrum of sorts. All the while, I was reminding her she couldn't bring anything like shoestrings, belts and razors. She couldn't have anything sharp or long which she could potentially harm herself. She was purposely bumping into me as she walked past me as I monitored her packing. It was as if she was trying to pick a fight with me.

If she wasn't at risk for suicide, why did she so quickly give in to my threats? She knew deep down she needed help NOW. In my opinion, she gave in out of fear of dying that day. This is an example of your heart and efforts paying off. We usually don't give ourselves credit for it because the tragedy was avoided. We so quickly forget that we succeeded at stopping a tragedy and wonder if we are helping.

Chuck asked her why she claimed that she wasn't drinking as it was clear that she was. He explained that we just wanted to help, so she should be honest with us. She said there were not even any bottles of alcohol in the house and encouraged him to look for himself. I think she was hoping his failed attempt would suddenly allow her to stay home by convincing us she couldn't possibly be drinking. He looked everywhere. Right as she was again claiming her innocence, he hit the jackpot and SO many glass tequila bottles fell out of the closet behind Lauren's hanging clothes. Clink, clink, clinkety, clinkety, clink. Chuck followed up with, "So tell me again how you aren't drinking." Jacque said, "I'll finish packing my bags." She stopped with the attitude. My sister was so weird about her bottles. She would pile them up as she drank them. Or she would hide them. I could never understand that. Like, wasn't the trash collection outside a hiding place?

As I drove Jacque to the hospital, I told her I would make sure Lauren was taken care of. I told her I would call her office, as most likely she would be gone longer than five days (it ended up being seven). I explained that I would visit her every day and asked if there was anything I needed to take care of for her. She begged me not to take her. She was crying.

Damn, I felt so bad. Who wants to put their loved one in a treatment center? Ugh. You feel like you are putting them in solitary confinement because they will be without all the things that give them purpose like their family, friends, and their job. What if a vital factor of their purpose is lost? It's crazy. The actual help can put them in additional stress once they leave and go back home. And what will they turn to? It's this civil conundrum. In the end, tough love wins. And it is TOUGH. Some of the hardest work I've done.

I also felt bad for her. No one wants this for their life. No one wants these problems. No one wants people telling them what to do. And no one wants to be the person telling another adult what to do. It's horrible all around.

Each day I'd visit with Jacque after work, but one night she asked if I wanted to come to her counseling appointment the next day. Of course, I said yes. Heck, I didn't even know there was an intake counseling appointment. She never invited me before. I felt so proud that she trusted me enough to invite me this time.

I arrived the next day for the counseling appointment. We were in this oddly tiny room that barely fit the swing of the door with a table and four chairs around it. At this point, Jacque was visibly shaking, but she wasn't that bad yet.

****

I just had to take a break from writing to burst out crying before I could continue. Then I called my editor.

I'm really struggling with telling people about this vulnerable moment of my sister's life. She finally trusted me and here I am telling the world. But, if I can help just one person feel human in this journey and have hope for a joyous life, I think she would want me to. The stigma of mental health and the idea that substance abuse should be private is deep within us through cultural conditioning. I hate it. I just want us to feel comfortable sharing our worst days or troubles. I want us to reach out when times are tough or seem hopeless. The only way I can be effective in bringing that change is by being the change. So here it goes...

****

Before I begin sharing the rest of the story, I'd like to educate you about blood alcohol content/concentration, known as BAC. This is done for medical and legal purposes.

According to the U.S. Library of Medicine[2], a blood alcohol test measures the level of alcohol in your blood. Most people are more familiar with the breathalyzer, a test often used by police officers on people suspected of drunk driving. While a breathalyzer gives fast results, it is not as accurate as measuring alcohol in the blood.

Alcohol, also known as ethanol, is the main ingredient of alcoholic drinks such as beer, wine, and liquor. When you have an alcoholic drink, it is absorbed into your bloodstream and processed by the liver. Your liver can process about one drink an hour. One drink is usually defined as 12 ounces of beer, 5 ounces of wine, or 1.5 ounces of whiskey.

If you are drinking faster than your liver can process the alcohol, you may feel the effects of drunkenness, also called intoxication. These include behavioral changes and impaired judgment. The effects of alcohol can vary from person to person, depending on a variety of factors such as age, weight, gender, and how much food you ate before drinking.

A BAC of 0.10 (0.10% or one tenth of one percent) means that there is 0.10 g of alcohol for every 100 ml of blood which is the same as 21.7 mmol/l. A BAC of 0.0 is sober, while in the United States 0.08 is legally intoxicated, and above that is very impaired. BAC levels above 0.40 are potentially fatal.

****

This is a close replay, as accurately as I remember, of a portion of that counseling appointment:

Counselor: Jacque, do you know what your blood alcohol level was yesterday when you checked in?

[2] https://medlineplus.gov/lab-tests/blood-alcohol-level/

Jacque: No.
Counselor: It was point .38.
Jacque: (no expression, no look of shock, nothing)
Me: (drowning and sinking slowly into my chair… at least, it felt that way)
Counselor: Do you remember coming here yesterday?
Jacque: Yes, I remember everything.
Counselor: It says here you walked in and signed in on your own, so you did that while at a 0.38 blood alcohol level. Do you know many people wouldn't survive that blood alcohol level?
Jacque: Yes.
Counselor: Can you outline a normal day of drinking for me?
Jacque: I wake up and have a couple of shots of tequila before I brush my teeth. I shower and usually have another shot. As I get ready, I have a few more shots. I bring the bottle with me. I take Lauren to school and then go to work. I take a few more shots in my car prior to walking into work. Then I come out at lunch and have 1-2 shots. After work, I have 1-2 shots in my car and go get Lauren. Then I finish the bottle at home. Sometimes I drink one and a half bottles of tequila. That's mostly on the weekends.

I was in a state of shock. It was as if the room was spinning but standing still all at the same time. I could hardly keep my head up, while my body felt like it was melting over the chair to the floor. It was like a slow drowning. I couldn't believe what I was hearing. Well, that's what it felt like. Completely overwhelming. Sometimes I wonder if the room really was that small or if the trauma I experienced made it seem that way as my world imploded on me. I thought, *How can I be of any help in this situation? This is way over my head. This is so much worse than I thought.* I thought I was maintaining a straight face, but the color drained from it in shock, which may have given me away.

What the hell! A fifth of tequila is 25 ounces! She was drinking 25-37 ounces of tequila PER DAY. (Side note: an average shot is considered 1.25 to 1.5 ounces of tequila so if we used 1.5 ounces as a measure it would be about 24 shots of tequila per day.) That's a lot of tequila.

My sister was at 0.38. Many, if not most, of us would not even survive that. She was walking and talking fine. Slurring a bit, but she was walking straight. I bet she could have driven too.

THIS. WAS. BAD. This was REALLY bad. I had no clue just how bad this was. WTH? How could I fix this? What were we going to do? How were we going to get through this with a good outcome?

When I went to visit my sister, each day I was so traumatized by the shakes she had as her body was detoxing. She was shaking so violently that her skin was visibly vibrating. You know how when you run and your skin bounces against you like rippling water? It was like that. Without alcohol, her body was going through a tremendous shock. That was so crazy. I'd never seen anything like that. I wouldn't comment on it and thought I played it cool. I was sure I didn't need to point out the obvious. But, oddly, maybe I should have talked about it with her. I mean that was her whole problem, not talking about stuff. And here I was unknowingly enabling her. Were we taught this as children, adults, students, humans? It's this behavior we continue to exhibit and assist. Allowing each other to avoid the uncomfortable even though the healing requires us to deal with the uncomfortable.

Every time, I left bawling, because I felt more and more helpless. I was not equipped for this. They don't teach this in school or life in general. I never told my sister I felt that way. I never let her see the fear behind my eyes and in my heart. I wanted her to see hope through me by not being shocked by all of this. I wanted her to think this would be okay, and that I believed she was strong enough to beat this. And I did think she would beat this, but I had moments of fear. I was scared out of my mind. She was my best friend (which I didn't even realize at the time), so who the hell was I going to share these very scary and deep feelings with? I felt so alone in this. Really, I brought that on myself. I didn't want to tell my parents how scared I was so they wouldn't also worry about me. I was the oldest. I was supposed to be dependable and resilient by cultural default, right?

Maybe I should have shared my fear with her to show her that being vulnerable was okay and even a good thing. I wish I'd known then what I know now regarding that life tidbit. Most times (and I'd venture to say all times) deep healing comes out of being vulnerable. An understanding of self can come from it. An acceptance of yourself as only human and that we are born to make mistakes. It was a missed opportunity, I think. Damn.

How was I going to save her life if she was using something that took her mind away from reason and care? Think about that. She was drinking to drown out her despair thus creating this alternate reality that everything was peachy-keen. But what happens when that goes too far and drops them into the very darkness they were escaping? It's like this funnel they spiral down so far that they can't get back out. Most days they get midway down the funnel and simply reach to the brim and pull themselves out of that funnel. But then there's the times they can't reach because they slid too far down. That's when they need that arm to reach down and pull them out. I couldn't be there 24/7 if she continued to drink.

This time, my sister left rehab at day seven and started taking Disulfiram. Disulfiram prevents alcohol from being fully metabolized. It causes nausea, vomiting, headaches, and flushing if you drink alcohol while taking it. Essentially, it is a deterrent from drinking because you don't want to feel like shit. Drinking alcohol while on it will actually give you unpleasant results versus the escape you are seeking. I don't know how long she used that, but she seemed to be doing well. However, there were times I thought she slurred her words with me while on the phone. I would bring it up and she assured me she wasn't drinking. Who the heck knows if she was or wasn't? Many people struggling with substance abuse are like magicians at hiding their abuse. You start to question your own sanity because of it. Like you know they are using, but they make you feel guilty for accusing them.

After 2006, my sister decided she needed to move to Colorado to start a new life. I opposed this vehemently. I straight out told her it was a bad idea. Here she was struggling in a sunshine state, and she wanted to move somewhere with long, dreary winters? In my eyes, this was a recipe for disaster. Plus, the guilt wasn't going to stay in Arizona. After all, Colorado sold alcohol too. Here she had this great job with a company that had supported her during her recovery journey, and she wanted to leave it? I told her the solution was counseling and professional help, not a new environment. You can't simply escape emotional turmoil by changing your surroundings. You might improve the appearance, but there's an inside job at hand that needs to be addressed. I was the closest person to her in that I felt I knew her the best, and this wasn't the solution. I didn't want her to be disillusioned. In the end though, I lost that battle.

Ultimately, in late spring of 2006, she moved to Colorado. One thing us Clifton kids were taught by our dad was perseverance and to be upstanding citizens, to hold a job and support yourself. We also all had great work ethics, which have really helped us in our lives. Having that going for her really allowed her to do something like this easily. She knew she could do it. So, of course, she quickly found a job and an apartment. She got help and support from our mom who lived there. We also had a younger half-sister and two younger half-brothers there, so she would have family support.

The trouble came when she started drinking *again*. That pain and guilt was still with her. My sister was spending $12-24 per day on alcohol, plus she smoked. I don't know how much she smoked, but a pack of cigarettes was probably $4/pack at the time. That cost with rent, insurance, and a hefty car payment couldn't have made things easy on her, plus she was raising a young daughter who required daycare. It was not like she was making a shit-ton of money. She lived a modest life but didn't have that kind of disposable cash to live like that long term. She ended up becoming a roommate with our younger sister, who was seven years younger than Jacque. Eventually, our sister moved out and Jacque had a live-in boyfriend. I don't know and/or remember the details of all of that, so I can only share the gist of what I remember to give you a general idea of her life when in Colorado.

Eventually, she lost her expensive sports car, an electric blue Mitsubishi Evo. That couldn't have been an easy life experience on top of everything else. My mom helped her buy a used car. I don't know what it was, but it ran well and was affordable. It was an outright cash purchase. I just remember my sister hating it. She was so used to driving a nice car that it was a blow to her pride. I'm sure the drinking and cigarette costs led to this repossession, but she didn't talk about that. Can you imagine the toll this self-destruction took on her self-love and thus her mental health? This was a downward spiral waiting to happen.

One day in mid-2007, my sister's then-boyfriend came home and found her unresponsive and foaming from the mouth. She was in the throes of alcohol poisoning. I thank God to this day that he came home when he did. It saved her life. I don't know if that time was a suicide attempt or not. However, I can't help but think most "accidental" overdoses or alcohol poisonings are a suicide attempt anyhow. You purposely chose to drink too much or do dangerous drugs. Perhaps not the case in a one-time trial, true accidental overdose, or poisoning, but in a case like Jacque, she always knew the risks. I feel every day that this was a suicide attempt for her.

Between Lauren being home during the alcohol poisoning and a reported incident where Jacque didn't pick up Lauren from daycare, the state of Colorado took Lauren away from Jacque. Lauren could not live with her. My mom filed for custodial rights and got them, so Lauren lived with her. Jacque was not allowed to take Lauren by herself. She could only see Lauren when Mom was home or around her.

Can you imagine that blow? Now you are so dysfunctional and messed up that you've lost your daughter. I'm sure she felt like a horrible parent. Your first daughter died in a drowning and now you've lost custodial rights to your youngest daughter.

That was when Lauren shared with the state that her mom was hiding bottles of alcohol in the cat litter box. Like WTH?! She was so desperate to hide her drinking that she actually drank or poured from bottles that were stored in a covered cat litter box. And here we had a five-year-old at the time who knew about it. My sister thought she was so sly, but even a five-year-old knew what was going on. Poor Lauren. Here was a wonderful human who couldn't be an easier child to parent or a kinder, caring daughter, and she watched her mom slowly succumb to alcoholism and grief. I can't even imagine what that was like to process as a toddler.

To get Lauren back, the state required my sister to be in a drug-alcohol program. It had mandatory weekly classes with random tests for alcohol. Of course, she did it. It was the least she could do to make things right. I'm sure though that this whole thing was crushing her spirit, her very soul. I don't know how often she went to see Lauren during that time, but I'm sure it was a lot. My sister just adored Lauren, and to be quite blunt, Lauren saved my sister's life for six years. She's the number one reason why my sister survived her last six years. I'm certain of that.

That's why I believe when Jacque was failing Lauren, she threw in the towel eventually. If she couldn't even do right by the one thing she was living for, what was her life worth? I put myself in her shoes and imagined that was a glimpse of her thoughts. But she still wouldn't talk about it. We wouldn't bring it up either. I'm sure that didn't help. No one wanted to talk about it for fear of upsetting her. She already had enough going on. We didn't need to add fuel to the fire. But maybe that would have made a difference.

That was ultimately the most important thing she needed. She needed to deal with the loss of Gwynnie. One of the gentlemen in my sister's program shared with my mom that Gwynnie was the one thing Jacque would never talk about. The one thing she needed to do, and she wouldn't do it. I'm so mad at myself to this very day for not talking about it all the time. For worrying about her comfort and not get it out in the open. That is my biggest regret.

Chapter 5

Seven Year Itch

In December 2007, Lauren was in Phoenix with her dad (without Jacque) for the holidays. Jacque's boyfriend broke up with her a few days before Christmas. My guess is it was simply too hard to live with an alcoholic anymore, although I don't understand why he didn't wait until after the holidays. That has always bothered me; it seemed heartless to me. I'm just the type of person that would have suffered through that time to keep the peace for the holidays. The two of them had been dating for several months and were living together. Why couldn't he wait? He knew she was alone. I'm not trying to place blame, but these sorts of things are a part of the "whys" that haunt you after. The "woulda, coulda, shoulda" regrets.

My mom had left town, I believe, on December 19th (so weird I still remember that detail) to go to Mexico for a high school graduation trip for our younger brother. So, she and my brother were out of town for Christmas. The winter that year was brutal, so Jacque and our younger sister, who lived three hours away in Yuma, Colorado, couldn't get together. It was blizzard weather, so it just wasn't safe to be on the roads.

Knowing she had no one to spend Christmas with, I asked Dad if he could pay for a flight to get Jacque to Phoenix. Although the two of them weren't talking due to a ton of money Jacque owed him for several months of car payments he made for her without payback, he said yes without hesitation. Unfortunately, I couldn't convince Jacque to come no matter what I said. I personally think that was by design. Nobody was going to be home.

Ultimately, all these circumstances led to Jacque spending Christmas and New Year's alone. I was so bothered by this. I kept begging her to come out, and she would continually say "no." She would tell me that she wanted to stay home and be with her boyfriend for Christmas. Of course, she didn't know he would break up with her right before Christmas.

My husband, Mike, and I used to go to Las Vegas for three nights every New Year's holiday. This was our 3rd or 4th trip with a group of friends to ring in 2008. As usual, we were having a blast with friends. It was no different than any other year...yet. My sister called me at about 10 PM on New Year's Eve. I was on Fremont Street under the light installation in downtown Las Vegas. All seemed normal. I asked her what she was doing that night. I was really concerned about her. She said she was fine and was "just going to be that old lady with the cat." I thought that was a bazaar comment. When I asked what she meant, she just said it was an expression she'd heard. When we hung up, she said, "I love you." I quickly said the same, but hesitantly. I'm so pissed at myself to this day for not reading that moment correctly. I didn't see it right in front of me. I thought she was turning over a new leaf with her new "cat" for the New Year.

You see, we never said "I love you" to each other. Ever. It was this weird thing in our family. I remember thinking, *That's strange that she said that*, and being surprised at myself for saying it back. Then I was even more surprised at how simple it was to say those words yet how guarded we were about saying it with our dad. Our mom always said she loved us, and we said it back, but not with our dad. I heard Dad say, "I love you," ONE time in my life. Once. And I believe that may have been the first and only time my sister and I said it. Thank God for that blessing. I find myself really embarrassed to share this now. Why did I not change that behavior? Would that have made a difference in our family story? I mean, you know your family loves you, so do you really need to say it? As I write this, it's October 2020, and I realize I just spent two years not telling my sister-in-law I love her. Why? I'm so guarded with those words even today. It's just silly. I should have known... but it was the new year. People change intentionally to better themselves. I continued celebrating in Las Vegas.

The morning of January 1, 2008, I started getting phone calls from Mom, asking if I'd spoken to Jacque. She couldn't reach her. My sister was calling me too, not realizing Mom had already called. It was like Mom had sensed something was wrong because she hadn't heard from Jacque. My mom did not have Jacque's apartment key, so she couldn't get into the apartment. Jacque had recently slyly collected that key, no doubt intentionally to protect Mom. I believe Jacque was supposed to go look at apartments with Mom and Mom couldn't reach her to organize it. I told Mom I would try to call Jacque and I reminded her that Jacque could behave like a hermit sometimes. Jacque and Jeff were always weird hermits. I couldn't tell you how many times I went to their house for a proof of life check because I was pissed off, she wasn't answering or returning calls. It was so annoying.

Secretly though, I was nervous. Did the thing I had dreaded all these years finally happen? Nah. That wasn't real life. My mind tricked me into thinking everything was okay to protect itself.

I called and called. Texted and texted. Nothing. I even called my brother Johnny to recruit him in the efforts. My mom had recruited my sister. They got nothing also. We called all day. It was late afternoon, and Mom went over there. Jacque's car was in the parking lot, but she couldn't open the door. Jacque's dog was barking inside. Mom called me and was in a panic. She said she was knocking and calling but no one answered. There was panic because Jacque's car was there. She didn't know what to do. She decided to call 911.

The police showed up and broke into the apartment from a window. They made my mom wait outside. I can only imagine the absolute buildup of emotion as she waited impatiently. She called again and said they'd been in there a long time and hadn't come out yet. She was crying and nervous. She kept saying, "This doesn't look good." Then she said the detective was walking towards her and she would call me back. She again was in a bit of a panic because Jacque wasn't with him.

I was in the Golden Nugget Hotel, gambling. I asked my friend if she would go back to my room with me as I took calls to help Mom and the family figure out what was going on with Jacque. As we walked back, towards the hotel lobby to the elevators, my phone rang again. It was Mom. I answered immediately.

"SHE'S GONE!" she wailed in a piercing tone, in complete shock.

"What do you mean she's gone?!" I cried.

"SHE'S GONE!" Mom repeated.

"What does that mean?!" I asked much louder as I collapsed to the floor as I knew what it meant. I could hear that same desperate dread in her voice as when Jacque was in that room on the floor in the hospital after losing Gwynnie.

"SHE'S DIDN'T MAKE IT!"

"I don't understand. WHAT DO YOU MEAN!?!?!" I shrilled even louder as I was already a sobbing mess.

"SHE DIDN'T MAKE IT. SHE'S DEAD!"

She's dead. These are words you can't comprehend naturally.

I was on the floor right by the hotel lobby in the fetal position moaning, "Nooooo! God, please no! Not her! Please take me! Not her! Please take me! Nooooo! Please make this not real! Save her! PLEEEEASE! Please! I'm begging you! Save her!"

I didn't even have to ask how she died. I knew. I'd already processed that at that moment, realizing she had told me she loved me. I then understood the sentiment and why she made the call in the first place.

My friend was trying to get me up. My legs wouldn't work. I literally could not engage them. It was as if my body did not have the energy, or my brain could not operate them at the same time because of the trauma. Or both. My brain was like, *Oh heck no. I can't make those legs work. I'm busy over here processing an overload of info.*

I could not believe what I heard. I just couldn't. I kept saying, "THIS CANNOT BE REAL!" I kept pleading to God to make this untrue, to take it away, to reverse it, and to stop messing with us. I was angrily blaming Him for allowing this to happen. I asked Him why He would let this happen to her after all she had been through, and why He would put us through this after all we had been through. I asked why He wasn't helping us and why He'd forsaken and ignored us.

We will get back to faith later. I want you to know I am on fire for Jesus now. My faith is infallible. I want to encourage anyone experiencing grief to hold true to your faith. Don't let go. Don't turn away as I did. Your Jesus,

Messiah, Buddha, Allah, Universe, Higher Power, etc. did not do this to you. I'll leave that there for now.

My friend finally got me on my feet, but it looked more like her carrying a wounded soldier. I could barely function. I couldn't hold my shoulders up. It was like being a stroke victim, temporarily. I lost function of my body. My entire body was hunched in absolute sorrow.

Mike came up to the hotel room. I think my friend called someone else to go find Mike in a poker room where he didn't have his phone on. Mike immediately wrapped his arms around me, and said he was sorry. After our hug, we started packing to head home early. While in the room, I called Dad and Johnny. I asked Dad if anyone was home with him. He said his younger brother was right there and asked why.

I said, "It's Jacque."

"What happened?" he asked.

As I started crying, I said, "I don't know how to tell you this."

"Oh noooooooo! NOOOOOO! NOOOOOO!" He started sobbing hard. I couldn't hide my own desperation and gave it away. Now, I was bawling. I felt so bad for my parents.

I don't remember much more after that. I vaguely remember calling Johnny and Jeff. I think I went into shock. I cannot even express the depth of this pain. I always knew there was this risk of losing Jacque to suicide, so I thought it would be easier to accept and understand if it happened. I was wrong. It wasn't.

There was this thing I read about parents who lose a child, that they were at risk for divorce and suicide within the first seven years following the death.

Jacque did get divorced, but I thought we beat the suicide odds at seven years and eight months. I literally placed my trust and relief in that article. They forgot to mention the seven-year itch that may pop up.

I don't remember the four and a half hour drive home much. I remember constantly crying and asking why in desperate moans. I just didn't understand. I couldn't even comprehend. I was starting to ask the whys and wonder what happened.

The next day I learned that she'd been calling a lot of us and saying her intended goodbyes. I mentioned it to my dad, and he said, "She didn't call me," as he wailed in pain. Later Johnny reminded him that she did call him during a three-way call with him. I guess it was brief and Dad didn't recall it because it didn't come with a goodbye. I explained that the call in itself was a goodbye.

Mom shared with me that when the officer came out to tell her, he got uncomfortably close to her face and said something like, "I'm sorry. Your daughter is dead." They must train officers on meeting you eye to eye with compassion when they tell you something like this. I can't imagine how hard that is to do.

I asked Mom if Jacque left a note. She said yes. As of the writing of this book, I'm unable to get this note from my mom, but, from memory, it was something like this with the first few sentences most likely being exact.

"I'm sorry. I can no longer live with disease. Tell Lauren I love her. Give all my stuff to Mom. I'm going to see Gwynnie. Love Always, Jacque"

That's REALLY close to the actual note.

She was so tired of drinking and being addicted to alcohol. It was eating at her soul. This disease had gotten so bad that she lost her car and custody of her daughter. Can you imagine? So on top of the guilt she felt with Gwynnie, she had that guilt to bear. My sister left one last item, a paper, along with old and new pictures of family and friends strewn all over the counter. It was like she was reminiscing and saying her goodbyes. It breaks my heart to know she was thinking of all of us tenderly, but desperation and mental illness was stronger than that love. Here was what she left behind with her note:

Her paper was titled "The Mask I Wear" but in researching, this is the actual poem. My understanding is she got this poem in the mandatory classes she was attending for addiction recovery.

Please Hear What I'm Not Saying

Don't be fooled by me.
Don't be fooled by the face I wear
for I wear a mask, a thousand masks,
masks that I'm afraid to take off,
and none of them is me.

Pretending is an art that's second nature with me,
but don't be fooled,
for God's sake don't be fooled.
I give you the impression that I'm secure,
that all is sunny and unruffled with me, within as well as without,
that confidence is my name and coolness my game,
that the water's calm and I'm in command
and that I need no one,
but don't believe me.
My surface may seem smooth, but my surface is my mask,
ever-varying and ever-concealing.
Beneath lies no complacence.
Beneath lies confusion, and fear, and aloneness.

But I hide this. I don't want anybody to know it.
I panic at the thought of my weakness exposed.
That's why I frantically create a mask to hide behind,
a nonchalant sophisticated facade,
to help me pretend,
to shield me from the glance that knows.

But such a glance is precisely my salvation, my only hope,
and I know it.
That is, if it's followed by acceptance,
if it's followed by love.
It's the only thing that can liberate me from myself,
from my own self-built prison walls,
from the barriers I so painstakingly erect.
It's the only thing that will assure me
of what I can't assure myself,
that I'm really worth something.
But I don't tell you this. I don't dare to, I'm afraid to.
I'm afraid your glance will not be followed by acceptance,
will not be followed by love.
I'm afraid you'll think less of me,
that you'll laugh, and your laugh would kill me.
I'm afraid that deep-down I'm nothing
and that you will see this and reject me.

So, I play my game, my desperate pretending game,
with a facade of assurance without
and a trembling child within.
So begins the glittering but empty parade of masks,
and my life becomes a front.
I idly chatter to you in the suave tones of surface talk.
I tell you everything that's really nothing,
and nothing of what's everything,

of what's crying within me.
So, when I'm going through my routine
do not be fooled by what I'm saying.
Please listen carefully and try to hear what I'm not saying,
what I'd like to be able to say,
what for survival I need to say,
but what I can't say.

I don't like hiding.
I don't like playing superficial phony games.
I want to stop playing them.
I want to be genuine and spontaneous and me
but you've got to help me.
You've got to hold out your hand
even when that's the last thing I seem to want.
Only you can wipe away from my eyes
the blank stare of the breathing dead.
Only you can call me into aliveness.
Each time you're kind, and gentle, and encouraging,
each time you try to understand because you really care,
my heart begins to grow wings--
very small wings,
very feeble wings,
but wings!

With your power to touch me into feeling
you can breathe life into me.
I want you to know that.
I want you to know how important you are to me,
how you can be a creator--an honest-to-God creator--
of the person that is me
if you choose to.
You alone can break down the wall behind which I tremble,

you alone can remove my mask,
you alone can release me from my shadow-world of panic,
from my lonely prison,
if you choose to.
Please choose to.

Do not pass me by.
It will not be easy for you.
A long conviction of worthlessness builds strong walls.
The nearer you approach to me the blinder I may strike back.
It's irrational, but despite what the books say about man
often, I am irrational.
I fight against the very thing I cry out for.
But I am told that love is stronger than strong walls
and in this lies my hope.
Please try to beat down those walls
with firm hands but with gentle hands
for a child is very sensitive.

Who am I, you may wonder?
I am someone you know very well.
For I am every man you meet
and I am every woman you meet. *

Charles C. Finn
September 1966

*On the version my sister had, the last line read "Don't be fooled by me. At least not by the mask I wear." And it showed up as an anonymous author.

****

Jacqueline Dorothy Mitchell
May 1977 - January 2008
Age 30

****

Suicide Hotlines in The United States

Crisis Text Line - Text HOME to 741741

National Suicide Prevention Lifeline 1-800-273-8255

Veterans Crisis Line 1-800-273-8255, Press 1

Trans Lifeline 1-877-565-8860 (for the transgender community)

Trevor Lifeline 1-866-488-7386 (for LGBTQ youth)

Soon to come!

988 Lifeline for Suicide Prevention and Crisis Response Signed into Law July 2020

Suicide Prevention Lifeline/Veterans Crisis Line with the simple, three-digit 988 phone number beginning by July 16, 2022.

Bonus Narrative 1

Lauren Shares Her Story

I'm Lauren, daughter of the one and only Jacque Mitchell. My aunt, Aunt Jenny requested I write a chapter in her book. If you're wondering if I know a lot about suicide, I don't. But I do know the side effects well. In Elizabeth Kübler-Ross' book *On Death and Dying*, she defines the five stages of grief as 1) denial, 2) anger, 3) bargaining, 4) depression, and 5) acceptance. I never realized until now that I went through all five stages. Recovering from someone's death is a cycle and everybody goes through it, but everybody's timing is just different.

My childhood is hazy, maybe because I blocked out the bad or maybe I just have a bad memory. But after days of my dad holding in a secret that would affect my life forever, he sat me down and told me one of the hardest things he ever had to do. He looked into the innocent blue eyes of his seven-year-old little girl and told her she wouldn't see her mom again. I had no idea what I was about to hear. Heartbreaking. His few words crushed my soul. Through his own tears and broken words, I looked up and said, "Like Gwynnie?" It was as though I understood, but he knew I didn't fully. That was why I didn't cry as much as you might think a child losing a parent would.

When my mom first passed, I was told she was sick, which in truth, she was, just not in the usual way that we learned in school. It was hard. How does a seven-year-old process something like that? Usually, a dog dies, or a grandparent dies first long before a child's own parent. I think I was confused more than anything, and that's what death leaves you with: confusion.

For most of my childhood, it was hard to talk to anybody about my own problems because it never felt like anyone would understand this loss. The loss of a parent is different from the loss of a child or the loss of a sibling or wife, so I never reached out to my family. In high school, years later, I found one person who understood more than anyone what I had gone through, Lily. She lost her dad about the same age I lost Mom, not by suicide, but the cause of death wasn't what connected us. It was that hole in our family dynamic, the loss of someone you looked up to. This is important to note because I now knew I was not alone in my experiences, and that the stages I went through were exactly aligned with hers.

My child's brain didn't truly process my mother's death until I was about nine years old. This is one of the most vivid memories I have.

The music blared in my dad's truck. I was in the backseat. We passed under the orange freeway lights, and all was good. I watched as we passed dozens of cars, none of significance, until I saw this one bright blue car, a 2005 Mitsubishi Evolution. Obviously at that time I didn't know what the exact car was called, but I recognized it as my mom's old car. My heart raced as if she was possibly in that car. I squinted to see through the tinted windows to see if it was her. Obviously, it wasn't, but for a few seconds, I was completely convinced it was her, so seeing that it wasn't, broke me. That was the moment I realized that she was truly gone. She wasn't just living a secret life somewhere else, or she wasn't working for the FBI. My family wasn't hiding her from me. She was truly gone. I opened up to Lily about this experience. I was thinking, *Wow, I must sound stupid. Like I for real thought for years that my dead mom was alive.* What I didn't expect was for Lily to say she had thought the exact thing about her dad for a long time. She swore her dad would at one point come home from being a secret agent or something, which neither her dad, nor my mom, would ever do.

A wave of sadness overcame me like no other that night in the backseat and I bawled my eyes out for days. I was depressed for weeks. I would never smell her, see her, hug her, or hear her again. All that time, I had been in denial. I denied the fact she was dead, and it took years for me to come to that realization. That was just the first stage of recovering from her death.

This was before I had even found out how she had passed. I didn't learn this until I was about thirteen. A secret this big was bound to be found out. It was not as if my family had hidden it from me to lie to me. They just knew it would be a lot to take in as a small child and planned to tell me later. As a tween, I was quite the snoop, and that was how I found out how my mom passed away. I knew for weeks before I had the guts to finally ask my dad if it was true, had my mom really committed suicide? It caught him by surprise that night as the words burst out of my mouth just as I started walking up the stairs to my room.

He sat down and told me the truth: the bipolar disorder, the alcoholism, and the depression of the loss of my sister. I probably wouldn't have understood it as well if it weren't for TV. At the time I was lost in this one TV show where one of the main characters struggled with bipolar disorder and depression, and it really reflected my own life. It taught me something that no one could've explained as well as they did in the show. I'm not saying it made me understand what my mom did, because it didn't, but it put some things in perspective. I was a mess, distraught, more confused than ever, and I went on a long, long emotional rollercoaster that even to this day, I'm still on.

Suicide leaves a wake of emotions that hurt like no other. The anger is overwhelming; for months I was pissed at my mom, mad that she left me to be raised only by my dad. I was a growing teenager with already enough anger as it was, but this anger was beyond control. I was angry that I couldn't have a normal family with a mom and dad, that I couldn't have a mom to go bra shopping with, that I couldn't just have family dinners or do all the fun things my friends did with their moms. I was mad that my mom had chosen my sister, Gwynnie, over me. I was mad that my mom had left me. I didn't ever tell anybody how angry I was because I didn't think they would have understood. All this built-up anger was probably why I lashed out as a teen. I was displacing my anger on other people like my dad or my friends. I should've talked to somebody about it because it can seem like other people won't understand, but those who have experienced such a loss, do understand. For a long time, I basically was just so mad I ignored the thought of my mom. I didn't look at pictures or enjoy talking about her, which just hurt me in the end. Every negative thought was a stab that made the depression stage more difficult.

Then, gradually, the anger changed. I started asking questions and going on those annual suicide walks with my Aunt Jenny, which helped a lot. Talking to my family about who my mom was and hearing their point of views made me come back to the realization that I couldn't be mad at my mom. She was dealt a difficult hand, one that I don't think a lot of people could have handled. The stories brought me peace, hearing about my mom in ways I didn't get to know. But with all these questions and stories, I was sent into a deeper stage of depression.

I felt lost in overwhelming sadness. I was sad that I would never get to know this amazing person my family spoke about. The stories just made me want to cry because I wanted to know that person, and I would never be able to. Since the time of my mom's passing, my memory has only gotten foggier and foggier, which is one of the sadder parts. Bold memories stick to the front of my mind as I grip onto them, but some things have just slipped away over the years. I was sad that I wouldn't get my own memories with her, that all I had was a few. I was sad I couldn't remember her voice, the way she smelled, or the feeling of her hugging me.

The one thing that still can make me more sad than ever is this one thought—that I wasn't good enough. It is this aching that you couldn't be enough for them, which is dark. It's something I hate thinking about, but it's a mindset that would crawl into my mind that I couldn't escape. I know my mom loved me a lot. I am reassured of that, but our minds can always go to the darkest places. For a long time, this depressing stage left me contemplating following my mother's footsteps many times. I was hurt. I felt like if I wasn't good enough for my own mother, I couldn't be good enough for anyone. This set off a whole other cycle of depression and issues of self-confidence. But anytime I thought of hurting myself, I thought of my dad. I thought about how much my mom's death hurt me, and how much it would hurt my dad if I did something like that.

I can't say that getting out of the depression stage was easy, it was one of the most difficult times in my life. Some days it felt like the plate I was given was too much to handle. There was never a day when it all just went away, it gradually just got better. I slowly realized that I had a great life, with amazing people around me, and I was stronger than ever because of what I had been through.

Truthfully, I am not sure I would have made it through without a person to be alongside me. Ever since I met Lily, we've connected so easily, we both can empathize with one another and truly understand what the other is going through. We both have noted the days that are the hardest: their birthdays, their deathdays, and Mother's and Father's Day. It's extremely difficult to put into words how relieving it is to have her, like the weight I carried by myself for all those years has been released. I know I am not alone, I am understood and heard. That's something I wish for everyone going through something like this, to find a person that understands your loss more than you think they do, to have someone that can cry with you and grow from the pain alongside you.

Another important piece of healing was listening to those who knew my mom. When I visited my aunt in Colorado, she told me stories upon stories of my mom. Stories that convinced me she was a good person and a good mom. Hearing about her was one of the things that dragged me out of the depression. Understanding her death and what brought her to come to those decisions was the way to acceptance. I don't believe there will ever be 100% acceptance. I believe there will always be cycles of grief throughout time because it's inevitable to not miss her. In time, these cycles of emotions are lessened, the pain gets better, and slowly the mind and soul are healed. I've learned to live without those who I have lost, and I know they are at peace.

My family, it seems, has been through hell and back with the losses we have felt, but somehow, we all are better than just "okay." We aren't just surviving, we are thriving because through our losses we healed and came together as a family to love each other, and to love those who are gone. My family is my inspiration for always wanting to better themselves and find ways of coping that are healthy and proactive to others. They have never been the type to shy away from the subject of those who have passed, which I am forever grateful for, so that I could hear and sympathize.

I don't know who has felt a loss like this, probably hundreds to thousands of people have lost their parents this way. Even more people have just lost someone significant to suicide, and no matter the case, I think it's extremely important to come together and love while you can, be kind, and always hug those you love tight.

****

I miss you, Mommy, every day. I wish I could sing Gwen Stefani with you one more time or pretend to be the Grudge to scare my aunt again. I wish I could sit in the bath as you rinse my hair singing "Lean Back." These are the memories I grip onto, the good and happy. I am sorry for the years of anger that I manifested at you. I wish you could hold my hand today as I step off to bigger and better things. You truly are a wonderful soul, a sunflower in a field of weeds. I love you and I'm glad you could go be an angel with big sis Gwynnie. Until I see you again.

Lauren Mitchell

Chapter 6

Why

The infamous suicide grief question: Why? Suicide is such a mind screw. It's such a complicated grief. You spend what seems to be your every moment trying to figure out the whys. The whys and hows will haunt you on the suicide grief journey. Please try your hardest to understand you won't know all the whys and hows.

WHY?

WHY did this happen?

WHY my sister?

WHY did she do this?

WHY couldn't we help her?

WHY wasn't our love alone enough for her to stay?

WHY didn't I see this coming?

WHY couldn't she get the help she needed?

WHY did everything play into leaving her alone and lonely?

WHY did Lauren lose her mom?

WHY is this happening to us?

WHY is this happening to me?

What the F? This is crazy! How am I going to process this? How am I going to live a normal life with the hole in my heart?

While I didn't know any of the answers then, I'll answer with what I have learned now to give you some early peace, however big or little that may be. Any peace in this journey is better than none.

WHY?

I will never really know. The sooner I came to accept that, the sooner I found peace in bigger nuggets. I can't know why because I'm not her. I am me. She was living through an internal civil war that she ultimately lost. I can never truly understand that war she fought, but I can understand it was her daily life. You cannot rationalize something that is not conventional. There's no reasoning with suicide.

WHY did this happen?

Because mental health is not understood enough to help people efficiently all the time. Because of loneliness. Because of hopelessness. Because of nagging guilt. Because of a broken heart. Because of substance abuse.

Because she didn't get counseling. Because when you wrap all these things up in a bundle, you get a mess, and this is the result of that sometimes. It's like everything happened all at once leading to tragedy at that moment in time.

WHY my sister?

My sister was sick and succumbed to that sickness. Was she even in control of her sickness? How could she be? The battle was in her ill brain, which she was also self-medicating (another mental illness).

WHY did she do this?

If we make decisions with our brain (a major organ in the body) and that brain is sick, did she really "do" this? Her brain was not serving her. Someone with type 1 diabetes is born with an ill pancreas. If they die from that disease, do you blame them and put action verbs on them? No, you have empathy for them because they were sick. How is a mental disease different? It's not. I never use the word "committed" or "decided" or "took" when I tell others how she died. I say she died "from" or "by" suicide.

When I put an action verb on my sister, I take away from the tragedy of mental illness because I place blame on her and not the illness. My sister had mental illness prior to losing Gwynnie. That trauma of losing Gwynnie then added to her mental illnesses through a broken-heart and alcoholism. Trauma-induced mental illness on top of genetic mental illness. We must give our loved ones grace and empathy for the struggle they go through and succumb to.

WHY couldn't we help her?

I did! Many of us go through years of battle with our loved ones. Give yourself credit for the time you bought them with your love and efforts. It did matter and made a difference. You can bet on that. You can't be there ALL the time. You just can't. You can't make someone happy. You can't will or make someone mentally well. Do not drown yourself in guilt. You are not guilty. Guilt insinuates you took part in their untimely death, but you didn't. What you are feeling is regret. Regret you didn't do more. But you are thinking of the things in retrospect. You know you could have helped because you now understand that in hindsight. The you before they died didn't know this information. Your regret is through 20/20 eyes. Those aren't the same eyes you had then. Regret is normal but learn to process the sentences prior to this. Stay away from the word guilt... you are NOT guilty.

WHY wasn't our love enough for her to stay?

She lacked self-love. It's impossible to receive love fully if you don't love yourself. That is an underlying problem of suicide... self-love. Our love cannot replace her lack of love for herself. She may even have felt guilty for the love we had for her as she may not have felt worthy of it. That feeling for some with mental illness can make them feel guilty about your investment in them. It's so sad.

WHY didn't I see this coming?

My love doesn't give me the superpower to know what she was thinking. She was also very good at hiding her pain. She had very developed defense-mechanisms in that regard. The poem she left even confirmed that she knew that.

WHY couldn't she get the help she needed?

She could but she didn't. And the times that she did, it wasn't enough. She needed more. Self-medicating with alcohol was only intensifying the problems. And, for many of us, insurance failed with the nonsense mental health coverage and restrictions. Between that and my sister's lack of getting more help, she wallowed in pain. I find it interesting that if you go to the hospital because you had a heart attack, they do everything possible to figure out what happened and what they need to do to fix/prevent future occurrences, so you don't die. But if you go in for a suicide attempt or suicide risk, they assess you and send you home too fast, because nothing is currently wrong after a short watch. No brain scans. No DNA test for medications to make sure you are on the best ones for your mental illness. No required follow up. No blood tests. Like what the fuck?

Did you even know there is genetic testing available to determine the best pharmaceuticals for your genes? I bet you didn't. Neither did I. Instead, they play a ridiculous eenie-meenie-minie-moe game when choosing medications many times. Hopefully this one works. Let's reassess in so many weeks (how long most mental illness pharmaceuticals take to kick in), and if it doesn't work, we will try another. And if that one doesn't work, we will try another. It's all so sad. All the while, you know you are playing Russian roulette with your loved one's life. It irks the crap out of me. Why not give the DNA test so we have a better chance at getting it right the first time, and then coming up with pharmaceuticals that are injectables like birth control solutions on the market? Then you don't have to depend on a person that is mentally ill to take their medications.

Why aren't they telling us about these tests so we can treat our loved ones successfully and faster? Many patients die by suicide while trying to find the right medication. I don't believe insurance pays for these tests quite yet, but great changes are happening in the mental health sector.

Jacque's friend showed me her DNA test results from one of her hospital stays. It was several pages long and impressive. I was so pissed, because Jacque struggled with medications due to the liver damage she had caused with alcohol abuse. This could have helped her. Why aren't we doing this for everyone? Why do we continue this medicine game in mental health pharmaceuticals if we don't have to? I'll never understand.

WHY did everything play into leaving her alone and lonely?

Life. That's just life. Maybe she was called to be an angel sooner than we wanted although I hate hearing that. Maybe the devil played his part in it. I don't know, but it happened, and we can't change it.

WHY did Lauren lose her mom?

Again, life. It's bullshit, but it's the reality of it all.

WHY is this happening to me?

And more life. We don't all get dealt shitty circumstances like this, but I know everything has a purpose and reason. Most of the time, we learn that later.

HOW am I going to process this?

Day by day, moment by moment, and always with love. I truly believe if we give ourselves the forgiveness and grace that God gives us, it makes it easier.

We are called to do that for ourselves and others... including the loved ones we lost. I must commit to going through this constructively.

HOW am I going to live a normal life with the hole in my heart?

Just as you do any other day but add some tears and scattered thoughts. Grief is the price we pay for love. Costly, I know, but so worth it. Love is a wonderful emotion, and there's nothing wrong with grieving the love you can no longer give your loved one. Why wouldn't you? Now that love is bottled up. Interesting, that it takes energy to love someone in this life, but seemingly more energy when they are gone now that you can't give them that love. It takes more energy to harness the love you can't give than to just give it. It's that longing and aching that love creates when they are gone from this world. Such a conundrum.

Is she going to HELL?

This is such a touchy subject. Originally, I wasn't going to write about it, but that wouldn't be very open of me. Also, I am sick of the shaming and stigma. We all wonder that, even those of us not sure about Jesus and the afterlife... like the what ifs. I think there are VERY few cases where a victim of suicide is not suffering from mental illness. And I mean VERY few. Would God really condemn a sick person? No. Would he condemn someone not in control of themselves? No. He gives them grace and compassion. He welcomes them into His kingdom with open arms.

And that's my final answer. I have no doubt. Jesus has spoken to me over the years. I know Jacque is in heaven. No doubt. Stop beating yourself up over this. Jesus would not send your ailing loved one who died of mental illness complications to hell. Do you really think our Father is like that? He is not. He is the most wonderful part of life. He is the greatest love story of all time, and I know that love is all-knowing with an understanding of mental illnesses.

What was Jacque trying to say in that poem? Was she lying all that time about feeling okay? Or did she actually feel okay at those times? Did she try to reach out, but I didn't hear her? I just don't understand how you can look at photos of the people you love and know they love you, and not be able to talk some sense into yourself.

I'm only going to share this next part because I know it will help you, the reader, piece together this story. I know curiosity gets the best of us, and I'm pretty sure it killed my sister's "cat" that we didn't find. We all want to know by what means a suicide happens. Ultimately, it doesn't matter, but I want you to follow this story, and I know that missing detail can hold you back in your thought train. I'll say it again: how our loved ones die, and the means, doesn't matter. It doesn't define them. What defines them is the love you have for them. The heartache we have is all the love we can't give to them anymore. The harder you love, the harder you grieve. Grief is the price of love in the end.

So here it is, my sister died by hanging. Notice I didn't say "hung," placing the action on her. Be kind and choose your words with grace for your loved one. That's the least we can do for them now after the struggle they endured. The strangest detail was that she was in her closet with her feet still on the ground. She used a bright pink feather boa. Honestly, what the fuck? Really? A bright pink feather boa? Good grief. Of all the sequins and girl stuff I own, a feather boa is forever out of the picture. She messed that up for good.

I knew we shouldn't have left my sister alone. My instincts kept telling me that. Loneliness kills. It really does. If I was there or she was at our sister's house, this would never have happened. If we were on the phone laughing all night, this would never have happened. If she had someone at her house to love or love her, this would have never happened. What was different was that she was alone, and that was the case in all her attempts in the past too. Mental health and loneliness do not mix. Humans need human interaction. Real live connection. Even a smile can save a life.

Now, don't get me wrong, I know there are victims of suicides that endured the circumstances I mentioned, and simply leave the room and find aloneness. Not all stories are the same. Different victims have different illnesses. People have different lifestyles, medications, diets, and other factors that contribute to a suicide. I can only share my experiences.

Now we had the funeral to plan. Another funeral for someone dying tragically before their time. You'd think we were pros by this time. but grief throws a huge wrench into everything. I created a beautiful video of my sister, which was full of photos. I burned it onto a CD and gave it to my family. The funeral was packed. Jacque was so loved. So, loved. But it hadn't been enough because she hadn't loved herself. It breaks my heart over and over even still. When we were leaving the gravesite, I noticed Cody, only eleven years old, wasn't following. I went back and he started telling me with conviction that he wasn't leaving without his Aunt Jacque. That was tough. As if this wasn't bad enough, I now had to help an eleven-year-old process the finality of this death on top of understanding the suicide. Hell, I couldn't understand it myself. I hugged him for a long time while crying with him. I kept telling him that I understood how he felt. How was I going to help him? How was this going to affect him in the long term? After staying there awhile and waving off others trying to help, he finally decided he would leave and keep her spirit with him at all times. One small moment of grief was tackled, but only a gazillion more waited for us. Suicide grief sucks.

Grief throws a huge wrench into everything. You practically have to learn to brush your teeth again. Hell, you need a checklist in your bathroom for showering, brushing, and grooming. Without a mirror, you can't remember if you even did those tasks. Sometimes you wonder if you wiped your ass, especially if you haven't showered for days. Sounds funny, but I'm serious. The seemingly simplest of tasks are daunting chores. The things we do without thinking are simply forgotten. Driving is dangerous in the early days of grief because you can zone out for the whole drive, wondering how you even got to your destination. Life is sucked out of you; it's like you're a zombie in a hardly functioning body.

I literally couldn't leave my house for weeks. I didn't want to talk to anyone. I didn't want to get out of bed. I just wanted to fall asleep and not wake up to this unbelievable living nightmare. Just like losing Gwynnie, I would wake up bawling as I got out of bed. I went to sleep every night with hopes of waking from this dream only to be let down again and again and again. I felt like it was a never-ending loop I would never escape. Like the movie *Groundhog Day*. Only this time I was aware that I was probably going to wake to the same reality every day.

Every morning I woke up crying, "Why?" Actually, it was more like, "Whyyyyyyyyyyy?" I was begging both my sister and God to answer this for me. I wanted to know why hearing my voice didn't stop her. Why didn't hearing other people's voices stop her? Why didn't the photos stop her? Why didn't she stop herself? And why didn't God give her a moment of peace so she could think rationally? Why was this even happening? How in the hell could this be happening? I had a love hate relationship with nights. I couldn't wait to sleep to escape reality and maybe even wake up to a miracle that this was in fact a dream after all. But I hated going to sleep because it meant waking up to crying, "Why?" in sheer confusion. I know a lot of people in grief have a hard time sleeping. I never really had this challenge. I think I'm a professional sleeper. Ha! Anyhow, I was able to sleep like a rock most nights. I had nights I struggled getting to sleep, but once I was sleeping, I slept well. On rare occasions, I woke up early in the morning, the racing thoughts made it impossible to get back to sleep.

I've always been thankful my body was kind enough to give me that sleep reprieve skill.

I found that many nights, I woke up at 1 AM and sometimes at exactly 1:11 AM. Many times during my days, I would see 11:11 and 1:11. My younger sister said she saw 1's on the clock a lot too. Sometimes I wonder if my sister died at 1:11 AM. We know she was up at one because she oddly called one cell phone of hers with the other. Maybe to check voicemail, we don't know why, but it did prove she was still alive on January 1. That came in handy collecting life insurance. Consecutive 1's are now a big part of my life. I feel they are the doorway to my angels and a sign of confirmation of when good things happen or that I'm on the right track. I'm given one little nugget of peace when I see them.

I had days I thought about leaving this world myself to escape the grief I was coping with. They were very dark and real thoughts. When you are in the pits of despair, it is very difficult to escape. You know what always stopped me? *Who's going to pick up my kids from school?* Such a silly thought because we had so much family support. They would not have been abandoned. So, that should give you a little insight as to the rationality and smallness of my thoughts. It seemed impossible to think of the big picture. I was tightly woven in a web of all-encompassing pain, and it felt like I couldn't get out of it. I remember waking up some mornings and sitting on the edge of my bed thinking, *That's it. I'm done. This is too much.* My next thought would be about picking up the boys. I couldn't let them down. I'd already let enough people down. They literally saved my life. That's why I highly recommend trying to stick with some of your daily rituals and chores. I also recommend adopting a pet to give yourself chores if you don't have kids. A pet can also give you something that you can give your love to, and they reciprocate that love in return. It's good to stay occupied. It's also good to run errands and get out to take in some fresh air. In your house, you aren't getting any natural sun either. If nothing else, go sunbathe for twenty minutes in your yard.

I stayed home for almost four weeks without doing any work for my employer. Shoot, I could barely shit, shower and shave... and wipe my ass. They were so gracious in just allowing that quiet time. Then one day I received a call from my counterpart in the company. She was in charge of managing the Super Bowl event cleaning and it was a colossal undertaking. She really, really needed my help. Super Bowl was on February 4th that year, but she needed me back prior to that to get organized and we started cleaning a week in advance. That call and responsibility saved my life as well. I was so preoccupied with managing people and tasks that I hardly had time to stop and breathe. A lot of times, I was crying behind my sunglasses and under my ball cap. Our entire team knew what I had come back from, so they were so compassionate. They would hug me; ask how I was and more. I was just so blessed to have them there for me. I was also blessed to be pulled out of my house even though I didn't want to leave. I'm all about helping people and, after my perceived failure of helping people in my family, I felt the pressure was on to help others.

Because I was struggling to integrate back into life and work, I started wearing sparkly stuff on my rough days. Since there were a lot of those days, I started collecting more sparkly clothing, especially with sequins. It's tough to have a shitty day running around like a lit up light bulb. That was very healing for me, but I didn't realize it until years later. I didn't even really process that it was a coping mechanism at the time. Coping skills are the hardest but most valuable thing you learn post trauma. Just be mindful about learning healthy ones.

I've learned a lot over the post-suicide loss years. By "learn," I mean to come to my own understanding. Although I didn't learn that until much later in my grief journey, I feel it's important I share it with you now. My opinion from all I've seen and experienced is victims of suicide are just that—victims. I believe they did not DO this to themselves. They did not commit, kill, or decide anything in most cases. They are not well. Their brain, one of the major organs, is not well. While your brain is responsible for making choices, it doesn't mean the person actually made them. For example, if someone dies from a heart attack, do we say they "heart attacked"? No. We don't put an action verb on the person, we put it on the heart failure. Shouldn't we do the same for the brain? Wouldn't you say, "heart health" and "mental health" are a fair comparison? You can make a difference in both even if someone was born with an illness through life choices such as diet and exercise, and the type of medication you choose to take. Why do we place blame on a suicide victim, but not a heart attack victim? Think about that. Shouldn't we have empathy for the internal civil war a mentally ill person is going through like we do with someone struggling with type 1 diabetes? If your body doesn't naturally create insulin, wouldn't that be the same as a brain not firing right or not producing serotonin?

The system failed my sister. Sure, she played a part, like drinking or not taking her medications. She wanted the right medications that would work. She wanted to be alcohol-free. She wanted to feel better. But none of these things were happening consistently. It was too many battles to keep up with all at once. She wanted long-term clinical help, but then who was going to pay the bills? What do you tell people about your disappearance?

If she continued with clinical in-patient care, the chance of her getting life insurance would be affected in the future. They don't have a statute of limitations on mental health care records. You don't get to hide it after, say, seven years of "good behavior." I hope in the future we can come up with a program where you can be an in-patient, on a work-release care. In that program, you get your records expunged after five years with a successfully followed treatment plan. The program can be utilized by anyone with insurance or not. Right now, you can go to the hospital in the throes of a heart attack without insurance. They will treat you and do in-patient care until you are better. They don't deny you care if you don't have insurance and say, "No, I'm sorry. You will have to continue with your heart attack at home until we can find care appropriate for your circumstances." If you go in at suicide risk, yes, they take you in no matter what, but once you are feeling well and not suicidal, they release you. Someone at suicide risk is not well in their mind and they can be very manipulative with their behavior in order to get out, especially if they didn't want to come in to begin with. It's complicated because you are dealing with an organ that is both part of the illness and part of being well. Care is getting better, but it has a long way to go. A long way.

Bonus Narrative 2

My Crazy Selfish Loving Aunt

You were always my favorite.
But you hurt me,
Like an arrow through my heart.
You were the one that made me laugh the most.
But you made me shed the most tears.

You were my constant comforter.
My selfless supporter.
Never leaving, always standing by me.
You were there for me when I'd fall.
But on that day, I was the one you forgot to call.

You and I were the Twin Towers.
But just like them, we were viciously separated.
We made toy rings around our faces,
That was our unity,
Best Friends Forever.

You may not have been the smartest person,
But you always had the answers.
You would stop anything for me,
As I would for you,
But I never got the opportunity.

We drove fast,
In your little blue demon.
We lived life fast,
Like there was something missing.
So, we tried to find it like Mona Lisa.

We educated ourselves every summer,
But we did it the rambunctious way.
We watched the yellow square guy and his pink star friend.
We were SpongeBob and Patrick,
But we didn't get to spend forever together.

You didn't have to hit the self-destruct button.
But you weren't mentally stable,
You thought there were no other alternatives,
But you left us all behind.
We were devastated and shaken to our knees.

You were selfish,
But you loved us all.
You were lost and in a deep-sea trench of despair,
But you'll never be able to make right what you did,
You solved a temporary problem with a permanent solution.

I don't know if I'll ever be able to forgive you,
But I miss you every day like the sun smiling in my morning.
I will always love you,

But I hate what you did.
I lost you and I can't have you back.

You were the sister I always wanted but never had.
I was the son you never got to raise.
I know you're with me every day watching over like an angel.
I'll be with you one day so wait for me at the golden gates.
So, here's to us Jacque, I'll always love you.

Ever since I was a kid I always felt like an oddball. Compared to others, I was "a little off." So, naturally, I always felt like no one understood me. Of course, your parents always try to do their best, but if you're really lucky you have that one aunt or uncle who really "gets you."

Jacque was "a little off" and that's why she was always my favorite. When we were sad, we reacted the same way, like lying in bed, eating our favorite candy, and watching the shows that made us laugh. She watched *SpongeBob SquarePants* with me on those days. Once I was older, I think she loved it because it reminded her of her first daughter. When we were happy, we laughed so loud enough to cause disturbances because being around my aunt was one of the few times I felt like me as a kid.

She used to have this Electric Blue Mitsubishi Evo 8. Riding in the front seat of that car are some of my favorite memories with her. We once got pulled over while racing around with her brother who I call Uncle Johnny. By divine intervention, she was so nice and polite with the police officer that she didn't get a ticket, and then we raced a little more before we went home. We waited a while to tell Mom about it. Of course, Mom would find out, but she never knew that every time Jacque took us out, she let us eat all the candy we wanted and that's the reason we kept visiting the dentist. Staying over at Aunt Jacque's meant pizza, candy, soda, and best of all, NO BEDTIME. We never had to go to bed if we didn't want to, which was a gift for me.

Another gift was the PlayStation with the game *Gran Turismo* that she and I would play together. I like to lovingly blame her for why I still can't let people win in the name of fun. Weirdly enough, she would outrace me the entire time and pretend to mess up at the end, so I'd win. For me, I'd thought for sure I'd won fair and square, which was exactly what Aunt Jacque wanted because she somehow knew I needed those small stupid wins. When you were with Jacque, you didn't have to grow up. She had this two-story condo with ceilings that must've been forty feet high. Not growing up meant I could throw my candy as high as I wanted and catch it in my mouth. Eventually, we all joined in, throwing it as close to the ceiling as we could. Me, Jacque, my brother Brady, and her then-husband Jeff.

When Aunt Jacque was around it was always good news to me. For me, the reasons she was always around weren't important to a kid who wanted nothing more than to be himself. Aunt Jacque lived and she lived a lot, she struggled with her own vices and the shitty hand that life dealt her. I didn't know that until after she was gone, and I was older. How was I supposed to know? Those moments I cherished as a kid were the only moments I'd have. Of course, when you find out that one of your favorite people in the world dies by suicide it makes you start to question a lot of things and feel things beyond your ability to process. If only she was still here, we could talk about it, but she didn't even want to be here.

Suicide is tricky as hell and if you've never been down there, it's hard to understand why it would ever be the answer. It's a sickness and without the right love and care, it grows strong enough to kill. You see, Jacque didn't know the pain she'd cause by deciding to leave because her pain was so horrible, she could no longer bear it. She'd struggled with drug and alcohol addiction, she'd been divorced, and lost her daughter to drowning and that was just the surface. She taught me that no matter what's happening, you can always be happy if you choose and try to. I also learned that happiness does not come easily. Just like anything else worth having, you must work hard to achieve this.

Losing Jacque made me question if I'd ever be able to come out of my shell and be myself. That made me go to places in my head that I never want to revisit again. When certain things happen, I have a hard time getting over it if I can't understand why it happened. I kept telling myself there had to be a reason for it and when you go searching for reasons day in and day out, sometimes you hate the things you find. I turned twelve the year she passed away and the years got so much harder to deal with. I struggled to pay attention in school, I got into trouble and fights, and I argued with myself and my parents. By the time I was about fifteen or sixteen, I started to understand why someone wouldn't want to be here anymore. I honestly believe the only reason I stayed was that I knew the pain. I knew the pain that I would cause others if I chose the easy way out. At that point in my life, the worst pain I'd ever felt and the understanding of where Jacque was mentally kept me from repeating her mistake. For better or worse, I finally knew why.

I was lucky enough to grow up in a big family that was close, and I always assumed, as kids do, that family would only die if they got old. Now I know it's more complicated than that. Jacque lost the battle in her mind in 2008 and it wasn't until 2014 that I stopped blaming her for losing.

I think of her every single time I look at a clock or when I'm in my own car doing stupid stuff I should get pulled over for. I know she'd be with me laughing and enjoying it. I wish she'd been there the first time I got my heart broken because she would've helped me carry the pain and we would've eaten candy and watched our shows. She'd tell me something that would give me my confidence back and she always made sure that I was proud of being an absolute dork. That was our thing. We were loud, weird, and goofy and we didn't care how much the world told us to stop.

She was the kind of person who could light up a room or make a horrible day feel not so heavy. It's not so much the memories that I end up missing, it's the way I felt when she was around and now, I had to learn how to get that feeling on my own, but it does come. That feeling comes back. When I was eighteen, I decided to forgive her for losing the battle in her mind and I was able to start winning the battle in mine. See I'd hit an all-time low mentally and emotionally. I didn't see value in myself, and I started to believe that other people's lives would be better if I was not around. It's one thing to hear about someone feeling like that but when you actually have those thoughts, it makes your vision of life so much darker. Once I hit this point, I finally got the answer I was looking for. I knew WHY someone could decide to just give up on the whole thing. I started thinking of ways to kill myself. Where could I do it? When could I do it? You start becoming engulfed in this toxic mindset that you don't matter, and no one loves you. Who would even care if I wasn't here? This was when I realized I couldn't do it. I had so much time left to change things. I had so many people who would help me if I reached out. My story is nowhere near complete, and I can be the one to change the way it's being written. That feeling comes back.

It took me years to forgive Jacque for what she did and all it took was hitting rock bottom. That's a joke and poorly timed cynical humor. We don't have to believe the story that makes us not want to be here. We don't have to wake up every day wishing it was the last time. How can I hold a grudge against Jacque for leaving early if I make an early exit too? I can't. I know that if I leave early, I'll be leaving so much behind. I know that if the pursuit of happiness never ends then I better get ahead now.

Happiness isn't something that's tangible. We can't hold it in our hands or tell you exactly what it looks like. For me, happiness is something I work at daily, and I know that I can BE happy if I decide to be. The universe is an ever-changing monster and none of our lives are pre-planned or pre-destined. We can manifest who we want to be and the life we want to have, and it won't be easy, but it gets easier the more we try. Life will throw everything it possibly can at you and sometimes we are going to get knocked down and then you try to get up. Nope. You try again. Nope. Eventually, you will get up, not because you have to but because you choose to.

In life there are seasons, and in our head, there are seasons too. When life sucks it feels terribly cold and we feel like we're going through winter but just like the seasons change, so do ours. The sun comes out and the ice melts, the leaves change, and you will be able to smile again. You'll be able to love yourself again which is the hardest thing to do. We are all worth it and we all deserve to be here, we are just designed not to believe it when we hear it from ourselves. Once we change the story, living with it becomes a gift instead of a burden and I want my life to be a gift. That feeling HAS to come back and I'll devote my life to getting it.

Cody Gibson

Chapter 7

This Only Happens to Other People, Right?

My dad made a comment to Chuck, who shared it with me. We were friends at the time, so he shared in a humorous can-you-believe-your-dad-said-this kind of way. When he shared the comment with me, I was so pissed at my dad. I came unglued. WTF! I was like, "I'm his daughter why can't he be on my side? It was like he was supporting Chuck instead of me. I know now it was just his way of coming to terms with not approving of our divorce as he liked Chuck.

Of course, I was so riled up that I called my dad immediately. That was my first mistake, not waiting to calm down. I don't remember all the details of that call. I just recall saying something like, "I can't believe that you would side with my ex over me." I don't even remember what my dad said. I probably hung up on him. After that, we didn't talk for a long time, not more than a year, but many months. It's interesting because my current husband, Mike, comes from a family where they don't do that. They would never hang up on someone. I thought all families did that, but my husband was baffled by this behavior. It was so common in our family, and when I talk to other families it's very common in theirs too. We are all dysfunctional families in one way or another though.

I hadn't spoken to my dad since I hung up on him. Here was this tough-as-nails man that raised me, who only cried when you'd be a weirdo not to cry. One day in September of 2011, Mike and I were sitting in the living room and my phone rang. I said, "Holy crap! Dad's calling me!" I kind of had a feeling of relief that he was finally calling to apologize. For my dad to call when we were not talking, especially when I was the one to start the non-talking, was saying a lot. I answered right away, and he was on the other end sobbing and whimpering like a child. I'll never forget that call.

I heard my dad cry twice in my life; once with Gwynnie and once with Jacque. So, I understood how bad it had to be for him to cry.

****

These are the moments I struggle to write about in this book. I had to take a break to cry before writing this next part.

****

He just said, "Jennifer, I really need your help." I told him I'd be right there. I literally put my shoes on and left. How could I care what I looked like? After Jacque died, I was so worried that anyone who was upset could die by suicide in my mind. I asked Mike, "Will you please call my dad and just stay on the phone with him until I get there?" I was really afraid. I thought I was going to get there, and he would be gone. For my dad to call like that! Think about that. People, and especially men, struggle to reach out for help. I can't help but wonder if that was the day he was going to die, but he didn't want me to have the pain of not speaking at the time... like he had with Jacque. I'm forever grateful that he allowed himself to be so vulnerable as to spare me such pain. Thank you, God.

I drove so fast. I only lived eight miles away, but there were a lot of lights and 40 MPH-zone roads. It felt like watching molasses drip. The adrenaline fueled by fear was so heavy in my foot on the gas pedal. I practically drifted on turns as I sped to get there in time. When I got there, I was so overwhelmed. He had lost so much weight. His eyes were so sad. They were so empty.

****

Another break. Nearly ten years later and I still sob like a child when I process this. I don't know whether to be upset with God that I wasn't there for my sister in the same way, or if I should be grateful as He spared me seeing her in such a mental condition.

****

I hugged my dad for a long time when he opened that door. He collapsed into my arms. I could feel his soul was at the pit of his being. He was so broken. I'm forever thankful to Jesus that he had the courage to call me. Every day.

****

Another break as I cry while repeating "every day," full of compassion for the pain he was in.

****

Every day, my dad was living in a silent hell. A despair that he felt there was no escaping. Every day there was an internal civil war on so many levels happening in his mind. Should I eat or not, should I sleep or not, should I shower or not, should I socialize or not, should I live or not? His pride was the only thing holding him back from getting help. That manly pride does more harm than good. Man-pride is dumb. Why is it considered admirable that a man suck it up and not get help? Just deal with it and "man up." Maybe this is why so many veterans, and first responders suffer for so long after what they've seen.

That whole societal-created mentality is killing more people than we even realize. Why do you think older men and veterans are so high in the suicide statistics? Because they think they'll be a wuss if they get help. I'm so over the societal "man-up" pressures. And that "man-up" applies to many women as well depending on how they were raised, including myself or for anyone who had different life circumstances or were brought up like a female veteran. Hell, anymore, it applies to just about everyone, but especially men and veterans.

My uncle lived with my dad at the time, but he would leave town on the weekdays to go to the job site and he would only be home on the weekends. So, for five days, Dad stayed home by himself, depressed and lonely. His favorite thing was to watch the news, more specifically CNN and MSNBC with non-stop rolling chaos at the bottom of the screen. All day. I kept telling him to turn that shit off, but he was addicted like many of us are addicted to our phones and/or gaming. It was his drug of choice—escape from your own problems only to cause problems later. What a shitty way of living.

My sister Jacque would purposely isolate herself because she was drinking and didn't want people to see that. But she would still call people on the phone. She would still be social and held down a job. She went to work, saw people, and laughed. How could I be so stupid? My sister had died from loneliness too. All the things that played into Jacque being alone ended up being a recipe for disaster. Then the same happened for Dad. I swear, loneliness kills.

I was still so depressed from my sister and so wrapped up in my anger at my dad, that I didn't even see it. I didn't see what my ignoring him could do to him. If anybody's supposed to know better, it would be me, right? It should be somebody that's already lost someone to suicide. I feel like it's our human nature to place more importance in being right and being stubborn, which is something we do to the people we love most. We don't even do it to strangers. No, we do it to our own loved ones. We're going to do it to the ones that we love with all our hearts. It's so dumb.

As I was hugging my dad, I kept saying, "I'm sorry. I'm sorry I haven't been talking to you." He was crying. His shoulders were completely slumped over. I could literally feel his broken soul. I knew my absence had played some part in his mental and physical decline. I guess I got him good. I showed him, right? So dumb. Nothing accomplished but heartache. Maybe he wouldn't have declined to such a point or not as rapidly. Maybe he would be more mentally healthy if I hadn't left him in social isolation. Maybe he was beating himself up for what he said because I wouldn't forgive him. Grief comes with a lot of maybes. Maybes that you can't get back to redo. It sucks. But please remember, maybes are regrets, not guilt. I didn't know. I wasn't as wise then as I am now.

That was a hard day as my soul went into a downward spiral in processing what part I may have played in his current mental state.

****

Another long break to cry. I can barely get through typing this as it comes with so many regrets in hindsight.

****

We sat down on the couch where I asked him what was going on. It was still so hard to understand. My dad owned two homes, both with small payments and one almost paid off. He paid cash for a new truck, it was only a couple of years old, and he took pristine care of it. He even kept towels on all the seats, so that they couldn't get worn down. The interior was still like brand new. His credit hovered around 800, so he could get whatever he wanted. The house he lived in just had a new man-cave garage added to it that might have been the same square footage as the house itself. It literally wrapped around two sides of the house. And that didn't include the two-car garage it already had. He owned two boats, and one was paid off. He had hobbies with lots of toys. He had the nicest camping setup and gear. He had a pension as a retired Teamster. So many people would love to have his retirement. The American dream. Retired at 55 with a home, money, and a pension. What more could you ask for?

So, I asked him what was wrong, and he explained to me that the house we grew up in had a flood. It was sitting vacant as he painted the exterior to rent it, and one of the toilet lines randomly broke. He had just finished sealing all the exterior wood trim on the house, repainted the entire house himself, patched some of the tile on the roof, and other odds and ends on the interior. One day he returned to the vacant home when he discovered two inches of standing water throughout the home.

He could barely tell me this story before he collapsed in despair. He said, "I don't know what to do."

"Well, don't you have insurance?" I asked.

He said, "Yes."

"What's the problem?"

He was just incapable of dealing with it. So, he said, "It's so bad. Jenny. I think it was like that for days."

Then he shared with me that his medical premiums were going up, and it was a substantial amount for a retiree. It was something like $300 more per month. He said, "How am I gonna pay for everything?" So, we went through one item at a time. I started asking financial questions. Afterward, I calculated that he was going to be fine. He wouldn't even be strapped for cash. That flood had just brought up so many emotions, and then he couldn't process much else rationally. It was like the entire world was falling apart in his mind. Truth be told, he had so much bottled-up grief. It made processing more difficult. More on that later.

"What if the premiums go up again?" he asked.

"Well, you don't need to worry about that unless it happens. They may never go up and you're worrying for no reason." He mentioned his boat payment too. He didn't need to get rid of it, but he'd already convinced himself that he needed to.

I told him we were going to help him sell that boat. I was going to have Mike inventory his hobby room. I told him I would handle the insurance and the house. Later in the week, he signed a full power of attorney to me, so I could deal with the insurance on the house because they were giving me roadblocks. I said, "You're not allowed to go over to the flooded house. I don't care what happens, you are not allowed to step foot in the house. I'll handle everything." I also explained that I was going to make an appointment for him to see a psychiatrist.

That week, Mike met with him and helped him catalog his hobby room so that he could sell stuff. It was interesting because my dad really liked type A personalities. He really, really liked my ex-husband, and Mike was an easy-going kind of guy. He was a great guy, but that was not the kind of person my dad was attracted to. Early in my relationship with Mike, my dad asked me, "Why are you with this guy? I don't understand what you see in him." I told him just because Mike was not a type A person didn't mean he was not a great guy. Well, a few weeks after Mike helped Dad with his hobby room and to sell his boat, Dad came to me and said, "You know, Jenny, I gotta tell you something. Mike is a good guy. I really like him. I was wrong about him." Coming from someone that hardly ever praised or made compliments, that was impactful! Although there was no "sorry" in it, I knew it was his way of saying "I'm sorry."

My ex-husband always got upset with me when I wouldn't say the actual word "sorry." My upbringing made it impossible for me to do so. What he never understood was even when he forced the word out of me, it meant so much less than the way I had tried to say sorry without saying the word. My "non-sorry" apology before was full of heart and a true apology with genuine remorse, but it was never enough. It was kind of funny because I never meant "sorry" when I said it. It was weird that my dad raised me that way. Because I was the same way as my dad, I knew exactly how much heart was in his comment to me. That healed a wound in my heart forever, and it's something I am forever grateful for.

I scheduled an appointment with a psychiatrist for him, and, several weeks later, I picked my dad up to go to the appointment, I didn't trust my dad to get there on his own. He was so afraid to talk about his stuff and be vulnerable. I knew he would make some excuse for not going.

My dad went into the room as I waited in the lounge. After some time, his doctor came out and said, "Okay, you can come on in."

I said, "Oh, no, I don't need to come in, I'm just his ride."

That was my dad's business. The whole point was to give my dad someone to let it all out to. The doctor said, "No, no, your dad wants you to come in."

I was trying to tell the doctor I didn't want my dad to feel like I had to be in his business. The doctor told me, "It's not really like that. Why don't you come in?"

Ugh! My dad was a mess when I walked in. He had obviously been sobbing. The doctor proceeded to tell me, "Let me tell you what's going on with your dad."

"Listen," I said, "I do not want to be in my dad's business. I want him to be able to come to you. And this is private. I don't know why I'm here. I just wanted to make sure he got here."

"Well, your dad wanted me to share with you," the doctor replied.

My dad literally sat a foot from me, and I just looked at him, thinking, *Here he is, a mess, like that day that I gave him a hug.* The doctor proceeded to tell me that my dad was really struggling with the loss of his mother, then his granddaughter, and then his daughter. So, all these women (one was a baby) had been tragically taken from his life, and he'd never sought professional care.

His mom was sick for a long time before she died. I was born in '74. I think she died sometime between '69 and '72. My dad had told me his mom was sick. At first, they thought it was the flu, and then hepatitis; later they realized it was leukemia. Back then, when you got leukemia, there was no way to survive that. It was a death sentence, and by the time they found out she had leukemia, I think she lived less than a couple of months after the diagnosis. She was mid to late 30s. My dad's father was an alcoholic and abusive. I don't know if it was physical and verbal or just one or the other, he never really said, but he was very abusive towards my dad's mom.

My dad grew up as a strict Catholic because of his mom. He told me one time his mom didn't like to be late for church because there was one pastor that was really boring. She would say, "Let's go, we need to get to church. If you make me late, we're gonna have to see the other pastor, and I'm going to be really upset." So, she would get the three boys ready (my dad was the oldest of three). I think that's why my dad left his faith. He was so mad that God took his mom and left him and his brothers with their alcoholic dad as their only parent.

It's interesting because I was never raised in the church. I remember my mom took me to church a couple of times when I was eleven and younger. When she left we never went to church with my dad, not even on holidays. It wasn't until I was older that I would go with friends on holidays. So, I believed in Jesus, but I had no idea what that meant. The understanding of it all was never instilled in me, and I never had a Bible.

I literally did not know anything about the story of God, Jesus and all that stuff. And when Gwynnie died, I was over that. I did the same thing that my dad did. I couldn't believe or understand how there could be a God that would take this innocent child. But now I'm a true believer, I'm on fire for Jesus. What I've learned now is there's evil in this world, and people die because of the consequences of evil. For some reason, our loved ones are called to everlasting life, and we will never understand the why of it.

Back in this psychiatrist room, I couldn't believe what I was hearing. Here was a sixty-year-old man, he was almost sixty, and he was still sulking over his mom. Here I was thinking he was just suffering from the grief of Jacque and Gwynnie, but his mom too? There were decades of grief held in his heart. No outlet but his own thoughts. I can only imagine what he was dealing with for Jacque, because he wasn't even talking to her when she passed. They gave him prescriptions for a few medications; I think one was for anxiety and another one for depression. We went to the store to fill them, and I took him home.

The doctor's appointment was in October. I saw and spoke to him a few times afterward. And we had him over for his birthday in early November, Thanksgiving and Christmas. I'll never forget Christmas. On Christmas, he was still so sad, not himself.

That day when he was at the house, I asked, "Dad, why don't you come stay with us? We have room. Just for a couple of months because you need people around you. You don't need to be home alone right now."

He said, "No, I got my dogs, and you have four dogs."

"It's not gonna be much different with two more dogs. Just bring your dogs over," I said. I get it, if you're an adult, you don't want to impose on someone else. You don't have your privacy like you are used to. He wouldn't agree to my idea.

We have this Clifton family tradition. It's a weird thing Dad instilled in us. I don't even think on purpose, but by accident. If someone's leaving the house, we always go stand outside on the doorstep, and we wait until we see them drive off. We don't just say bye and they leave out the front door. We walk them out and watch them leave. We physically see them off safely.

As I was standing at the doorstep, I watched as he walked out to his truck and…

****

Here come the tears again.

****

His shoulders were so hunched over. His actual stance was screaming depression and sadness. I didn't know what else to do. You can't be there all the time. And oddly, I didn't think suicide was a risk because no one thought they were going to have two suicides in the family, right? I thought, *There's no way I'm gonna lose a niece, lose my sister, then another family member.* I just didn't know. I remember I came inside and said, "I don't know what else to do, Mike. I tried getting him to stay here. He was so sad walking out to his truck. Now, he's going to go home alone."

In the meantime, I was still dealing with the flood, and his house was coming along great. We were getting all new cabinets, door jambs and baseboards throughout. It was actually a great thing. A $1,000 deductible, and it was practically a complete remodel. I couldn't believe it. This was awesome! We got new carpet in all the bedrooms. It was a completely refurbished home.

Then the contractor called me and said, "We have a problem."

I asked, "What? What's the problem?" It turned out they accidentally broke the main island countertop, and it was an old yellow Formica 70s countertop that you couldn't get anymore. I jokingly but seriously said that it sounded like their problem and a good thing for me. So, we got all new kitchen countertops too! I kept my dad informed and even this great news wasn't enough for him.

Sometime in the following months, my dad said he wanted to put a will together and wanted to add me to his bank accounts. He claimed that this way I could handle all his affairs while he got better, including any payments that were needed for the house remodel. I could totally understand the bank account thing, but now a will too? I didn't like that at all. I called my brother and said, "Hey, you need to come out here. Dad's talking crazy shit. He wants to do a will and all this stuff, and I feel like I should do it for him, so he has peace of mind. But in this condition, I think it's a bad idea." My brother called my dad and then called me back. He said he thought it was fine to do it, and that Dad was just trying to be responsible. He also thought that adding me to the bank account and creating a simple will would bring peace of mind to Dad in his progress of getting his affairs in order.

When my dad originally called me crying, after I went over there, I asked my brother to come out from San Jose to stay with my dad for a while. My brother came out quickly and stayed with my dad for a week to keep him company and help him with hope. Of course, my uncle was still there on the weekends, but we felt Dad needed someone there around the clock.

I pulled a simple three to four page will off the internet, giving all assets to me including estate representative as per me and Johnny's discussion to make things easier in probate should that ever occur. I printed it out. Dad and I went to the bank to get it notarized. During that same visit, we added my name to his bank account, and we linked my online banking to his account. I could tell that it really gave Dad some peace of mind. He had a little pep in his step as we left the bank. We made him a copy and he gave me the original. That same day, Dad gave me the codes to his safes in case I ever needed them. That made me nervous, but Johnny assured me it was okay.

Mike's mom died on July 6, 2010. Her estate was finally wrapping up at the end of December 2011 and the beginning of January 2012. Mike was packing up her house and my dad was calling him, asking if he needed help packing and moving. Mike said no for two reasons. One, he was processing his own grief as he packed up his parents' home, and it was better he did that alone. Two, my dad was so negative. Mike was already dealing with a lot. He didn't want to listen to my dad complain and bitch the whole time on top of that. I didn't blame him. I totally got it. I think my dad asked about helping for two or three days.

I was on vacation during the New Year's week of 2012. I always took a vacation during my sister's death anniversary on January 1. I had sold a big contract in a downtown Phoenix hotel, and it was starting soon. Even though I was on vacation, I had some prep stuff to do, so I was working while on vacation on January 4th. I was in the basement at the hotel, and I never had phone service when I was down there. I was walking in the basement, and my phone started ringing. I thought, *Oh my gosh, how is my phone ringing?!* I stopped in my tracks and pulled my phone out of my pocket. The number was blocked, so I picked it up. The man on the other end of the line identified himself as deputy so-and-so with the Maricopa Sheriff's Department. Then he asked if I was Jennifer Ann Gibson. *WTF? Why is he using my full name with my full middle name, not middle initial?*

I immediately went into self-defense mode. The last call I received like that was when Gwyneth passed away. As if I didn't hear him the first time and to maybe create a different reality, I asked, "Who is this?" with a get-the-hell-outta-here-with-your-prank-call attitude. He again said he was with the sheriff's department. He asked if I was related to John Louis Clifton. I quickly said yes and asked if everything was okay. He said, "We need you to come down to the sheriff's department." He proceeded to tell me to meet at the crossroads which happened to be 25 miles from where I was located. He asked if I knew where that was. I responded, "Yes."

By this time, I was against a wall and had slithered down on my back to a sitting position. My hand was on my forehead as I realized how bad this might be. I explained to him that I was kind of far away and asked if he could tell me what was going on and if my dad was okay. He said that it wasn't time-sensitive, and they could wait for me to get there. He said not to rush. I said, "Okay, but is everything okay? Is my dad, okay?"

"We need you to come out here so we can talk with you," he responded.

"What's going on?" He wouldn't tell me. I told him I'd be on my way as panic and anxiety quickly took over my body like 1,000 spiders crawling on me all at once. I hung up.

It was so wild. I could never get phone service in that basement and that call came through. That's God and his miracles.

At this point, my ears were ringing loudly, and my brain was so foggy. I almost couldn't hear my own thoughts. It was like a very loud trumpet was quietly disrupting every thought I had. I couldn't complete my thoughts, because a new one would start. I was trying to find my way out of a basement I knew so well, but I was lost and discombobulated as fear rose in my body and mind. A hotel employee who knew me saw that I was crying and in bad shape. He grabbed me at my waist and got under my shoulder as he felt I may collapse, and he was right. He asked if he could call someone to help me. All the while, I was calling Dad's phone so many times, but he didn't answer. I was speaking to myself, audibly begging Dad to answer his phone as my soul sensed how bad this could be. I was thinking that maybe he got in an accident, or maybe had a heart attack from such poor care of his body while being a heavy smoker. I was also cursing the universe for allowing another call like this to come to me. I was just so undone. A mess.

Once I got outside of the building, I called Mike and filled him in about the call. I kept telling him that I didn't think this was good. I told Mike, "I've been calling over and over and over, and he's not answering." Panic rose in my voice and tears streamed down my face. My insides felt like water flowing over my skin and my insides were going with it. My stomach felt desperately empty. Since your stomach produces more serotonin than your brain, of course, I was feeling most of the panic in my stomach. As Mike realized the state I was in, he said, "Just wait, and I'll come pick you up, and take you there." But I wouldn't have it. There was no time for delay or waiting. I had to get there. So, Mike left work and we both drove there separately.

I called my brother and had the same conversation with him, and he was trying to assure me that I may be overreacting although he understood why. He was trying to get me to calm down, and he stayed on the phone with me the whole drive. He continually asked me to drive safely and check my speed. I was bawling. My eyes were so swollen I could barely see through the small opening and the constantly welled-up tears. I was reminding my brother of the similarity of this call and the call I got from the hospital with Gwynnie and explaining why this made me think that this was not going to be good. I shared that I couldn't believe after all we had done to help him and the work he had done to retire comfortably, that he may not even be able to enjoy it. Of course, Johnny told me not to assume the worst. As I was doing the math, I was getting angry with Johnny because he wasn't doing the math. It was not the hospital calling me. It was not the paramedics calling me. It was not the police calling me. He was not in jail, or he would be calling me. He was not answering his phone. A damn deputy was calling me from the building while sitting at his damn desk… without Dad there. This. Was. Not. Good. Johnny knew too but was trying to get me there safely through false hope.

Mike and I met each other there. We hurried inside and were escorted to an office with the deputy in it.

****

Here go those tears again. And I thought writing a book about this would be easy.

****

We sat down together, and he looked me in the eyes. The deputy simply told me that my dad was dead. He then said it was suicide at his home, and he was found by a neighbor. He explained that my dad left his license on a table with the will showing my full name listed. It wasn't until a day later at his house, I saw that he also left a convenient sticky note with my phone number.

As the deputy was talking like the teacher in *Charlie Brown*, I immediately fell into this side dream, remembering that Christmas day with his slumped over shoulders, walking to his car. I saw all the signs and I failed… again. I failed him. I failed her. He had been crying out in so many ways. Jacque had been crying out in so many ways too. Even after her, I didn't or wouldn't see it for what it was or could be. I did that dang will, and put myself on his bank account, giving him peace of mind in leaving us with an easy to settle estate. He'd been calling to help Mike for days. He had hardly eaten. He didn't enjoy going out with friends. He had called me bawling months ago, and I still couldn't see it. I was so blinded by the idea of how crazy it sounded to have two immediate family suicides.

That was on January 4th, but my dad actually passed on January 3rd, just two days after my sister's anniversary. Maybe that set him over the edge. Here he was processing all this life stuff and then that date came around. That pain he coped with privately. He and Jacque weren't talking when she died. As if suicide wasn't bad enough in denying you closure, but they also hadn't been talking. I can't even imagine.

****

I originally didn't want to put this in the book, but I want to help all readers understand that everything you feel and do is okay and NORMAL. So here I go with full shame. I kept calling my dad an "asshole." I was so mad. Mike even asked, "Will you please stop calling him that?" I was so mad though. I did it in front of the deputy, on the phone with everyone and in person with everyone. How could he do this to us? To me? I was alone here in Arizona. No other sibling here in the state to help with the affairs of all of this. This was so messed up. I'm embarrassed to even think about my name calling towards my dad in his state of despair. I've learned to give myself grace though. We think, say, and do weird stuff in times of crisis and shock. Did you know that many officers pee and/or poop themselves in times of needing to draw and/or discharge their weapon? Yup. They don't talk about that, but it's true. It's a true fight-or-flight moment in which they don't have an option to fly away. They must brave the moment, and oftentimes it comes with involuntary bodily functions. I figure, if they get grace, I can give myself grace too.

****

Mike and I went home from there. People were so nice. It was incredible how wonderful people were in a time of despair. I worked for this employer when Jacque died, and they catered the gathering after the funeral. I still worked for the same employer when Dad died. The general manager and longest tenure co-worker/friend came to my house immediately. They were the first at my house. I've always thought that was so sweet. A quick thank you to Jonathan, Jennifer, and Maria for that moment of kindness. They literally dropped everything at work midday and drove clear to my home, and it was quite the drive from the office. I am forever grateful Jesus gave me such a wonderfully supportive employer at such a time as that.

I just couldn't catch my breath. It didn't seem real. I kept telling myself, "I'll wake up tomorrow because this is not real." I begged, "Pleeeeeease, let this be a dream." It's funny because I didn't think I had faith in Jesus, but the whole time I was talking to Jesus. It was like suddenly He existed because I just cried out to Him. That's the true Holy Spirit in you coming out in your time of need.

All these people came over and I don't even know who anymore. I don't remember calling my brother. I don't even know if I'm the one that called him. I have a lot of memory gaps, there's just a lot of stuff I wish I remembered more so I could write about. Much of that time is such a daze. I just remember thinking, *How could my dad do this? Four years later, almost to the day of my sister*? What a great way to ring in every New Year for our family in the future.

When I was at the Sheriff's Office, I asked the deputy how my dad did it. He proceeded to tell me Dad was in his backyard under the citrus tree. I found out later from the neighbor that they found him and that his knees were on the ground. I don't understand how my dad did this. When my sister died, her feet were on the ground too. Here they were, still connected to Mother Earth and still too ill to come out of their trance of despair. So confusing and heart-wrenching.

My dad was outside. He had gotten one of the many ropes out of a container in his garage. The lid was left open even. He went outside, got on his knees, and hung from the citrus tree. In the neighborhood, they didn't really have fences and gates around their yards. They had pony walls that were about 1-2 feet tall to mark their yard and keep their dogs within their bordered territory. So, neighbors could walk through each other's backyards. It was cold that morning. My dad's neighbor across the street decided to walk between the homes instead of being on the sidewalk. She said she saw my dad, and she knew what it was. She said she wouldn't even go near him. She was screaming from outside of the pony wall, but no reply.

****

Isn't that ironic? It keeps bringing me back to my thoughts during this. I wouldn't let myself get too close to what I thought might be the risk. Didn't want to think or say "suicide" as if not confronting it would stop it from happening.

****

"John! John! John!" the neighbor screamed. There was no reply as he was slumped over. She ran around the other side of the yard where she could see his face, and then she knew what was wrong. She ran home to call 911. I felt so bad for her. She was ninety years old. She lost her first husband to suicide. They were literally eating dinner, and he got up from the kitchen table without saying a word and died by hanging in a closet. She didn't even know where he went. They weren't arguing, nothing. She had no clue why. Can you imagine? Here was this woman who lost her first husband to hanging, and then she found my dad. I often wonder why God did that. Wasn't what she went through already enough? Now she had to find her neighbor that she had a little crush on? Yes, she had a crush on Dad. She came straight out and told him, but he was tied up in the whole she-was-old-enough-to-be-my-mom thought.

Dad didn't leave a note. I have two suicides, one with a note, one without. Neither is better than the other. Just different. Do I really want a note from someone in such a state? This isn't a rational act (in most cases), so you are getting an irrational thought-process note. But, if you were never aware of their mental health decline, life problems, or suicide risk, maybe it would give you some closure, some insight despite the irrationality of it. Who knows? But I want you to know that I have both circumstances, and I like both and I dislike both. Don't beat up the situation if you didn't get a note.

Don't beat up the situation if you got a horrible note. Let it just be. It's a part of the story, but not a determining or judging part.

You're probably wondering, "What do you mean by 'in most cases?'" I'll tell you but remember this is my opinion and not clinical data, that I know of. I think it *may* be rational in a case such as a terminal disease or illness. Especially if that illness comes with a lot of pain and suffering on the final journey, regardless of whether it is short or long-term. Without legal assisted suicide options, I can see how that may be rational. We do it for our animals, for crying out loud. They are suffering and we save them from the unnecessary journey of pain to the inevitable outcome. We give them an act of kindness out of compassion. Is it necessary to make them suffer? They already have to say their goodbyes and make peace with things undone, which is mental suffering already. Why force them to physically suffer as well? Why can't we allow the same compassion for human life? How is allowing someone to leave to avoid pain any different than allowing someone in a long-term coma to die? Then there's the matter of dignity, which is a whole other subject, but do we really need to let someone wither away to nothing before they die? I think that's absurd. That's my rationale behind rational suicide, for what it's worth.

My dad had everything you would need in retirement and more, but it wasn't enough. It wasn't good enough. You know why? Because happiness comes from the inside. That was what did it for me. That was my awakening, about a year after my dad died. That was when my real healing started.

****

John Louis Clifton
November 1955 - January 2012
Age 60

****

Suicide Hotlines in The United States

Crisis Text Line - Text HOME to 741741

National Suicide Prevention Lifeline 1-800-273-8255

Veterans Crisis Line 1-800-273-8255, Press 1

Trans Lifeline 1-877-565-8860 (for the transgender community)

Trevor Lifeline 1-866-488-7386 (for LGBTQ youth)

Soon to come!

988 Lifeline for Suicide Prevention and Crisis Response Signed into Law July 2020

Suicide Prevention Lifeline/Veterans Crisis Line with the simple, three-digit 988 phone number beginning by July 16, 2022.

Chapter 8

Grief Epiphany

History just seems to keep repeating itself. My dad wasn't talking to my sister before and up to when she died. I wasn't talking to my dad for many months up to four months prior to his death. Those very voids of relationships may have or probably were huge parts of their mental health decline. I have a family member now that's not talking to me over a foolish and stupid thing I did, and worse I did it on a social platform. It wasn't intended to hurt, but it hurt this someone. I apologized. I tried to call but no answer. I texted. I messaged. They say they have accepted my apology but are still not talking to me. I've never once done this person wrong. One mistake and I'm not worth having in their life. What did I do about it? Not talk to them either. None of us have learned a damn thing, or at least not enough to forgive AND/OR let go.

But this is what our family does. It's learned behavior. Shoot, I still do it, and I definitely know better. I have three other family members not talking to me and I don't even know why. I literally did nothing wrong. I'm just so mad and hurt that people would do this to me. Why can't families communicate? I feel betrayed now, so I've joined the band wagon. I'm so tired of being let down that now I'm guarding myself from people I love, and that's toxic too. I can't even freaking learn to change myself. It's all just so messed up. And it seems like what happened with Jacque and Dad. Toxic behavior unnoticed, and/or unaddressed, and/or unchanged.

I was so angry with my dad about the way he died. I just couldn't understand. One of the biggest things about suicide is you take it personally. I wondered how in the heck he could do that to me. I thought, *That's so mean to do this to me.* I spent a year sitting with that anger towards my dad. While I had the same thoughts about Jacque, it wasn't so much directed at her, because I had a lot of compassion for my sister. I didn't want to judge her because she lost her first daughter. Still a part of me questioned, *How could she do that to her new daughter?* And then, *How could she do this to me?* But I gave her so much grace under the circumstances.

It's interesting that I didn't look at Dad's grief the same way. My sister lost her daughter, so naturally she was devastated. My dad also lost his daughter, and I didn't give him the same compassion to understand his devastation. I felt so bad for Jacque losing her daughter after spending time with her for only fourteen months. My dad had a daughter for thirty years. He died only four years after her, and I still didn't think that he might be in pain. And thinking about it more, he had her for thirty years! He knew her and loved her for so long. Hell, he lost his granddaughter too. I spent so long in that shallow way of thinking. Pain is pain… it doesn't matter whether it's fourteen months or thirty years. Why did I never give him that compassion?

Maybe I could have been there for him on a deeper level. Maybe I could have talked more directly about Jacque's suicide. I don't know why I never processed it as the loss of a child for him. It was as if her being an adult somehow made me miss that puzzle piece. Interestingly enough, I still do that. I sometimes don't give my dad the same grace for losing his child. I don't know, maybe some of it is because I wondered, *What about us?* He just left us for this one (Jacque) that does not live with us anymore. *Why would he do that?* These were some of the thoughts I was attempting to process in my head.

For over a year, I didn't have a nice thing to say about my dad and suicide together. I had a lot of nice things to say about Dad, but not about Dad and suicide. I thought it was bullshit. How could he do that to us? And for crying out loud, my sister died on the first of January, and then my dad did this on the third. Come on! Why would he do that? Our family was so raw in grief at that time of year. That was just two days after my sister. Are you kidding me right now? I was so mad.

Then I realized, it made sense. It was raw for him too.

I'm not saying all parents are at risk of suicide after losing a child. Most of us are of sound minds and can process this grief. It's a real bitch of time, but we can and do get through it. I don't know what goes bad with a few of us. It is a sick, untreated brain of sorts. We must get ourselves help even if it's just a friend we vent all this shit to.

As a family, we talked about Jacque often. We didn't want her to be a long-lost memory. Dad didn't really talk about her though. It wasn't that he ever said, "I don't wanna talk about this." It just didn't seem to be a topic he ever took part in. Like don't talk about it, and no one will get hurt. But the opposite is true; talk about it *so* no one gets hurt.

Of course, he never went and got clinical help. I should have known he needed help because I needed help. I was so wrapped up in my own pain and emotions of it all that I forgot he was in the fallout too. Suicide grief, or any grief, is a challenge in any family. How are you supposed to be there for someone else when you are barely doing it for yourself? You can't even see past your own pain, and you aren't whole enough to be that foundation. That's why I firmly believe the whole family needs to get into counseling individually when someone dies.

Once I had natural compassion for my dad, similar to my sister, I realized Dad did not do this. He was not in his right mind to do this. If he was in his right, rational mind, he would never do this and leave the two of us in this emotional turmoil. So, I thought maybe people don't "make a decision." Maybe, they don't "decide" anything. Maybe your brain, in very odd circumstances, starts doing its own thinking. Like your other major organs, maybe it can get to a point of functioning on its own without your conscious drive (although it does function on its own mostly). Maybe it cuts off your conscious will to live to mediate pain. Take your heart for example. If someone has congenital heart failure, and their heart starts not functioning well, then it gives out, and ultimately stops. Is that much different? I don't think so. Both are organs not serving the body, right?

That's why I refuse to use those action verbs; *decided, chose, took, hung*. I can't bring myself to place blame on them. Life circumstances and disease took over their brain. They say trauma causes inflammation in the brain, and maybe suicide is a symptom. Who knows? But, for me personally, I no longer blame them. I've accepted what's happened. My wish is they would have sought out clinical help, and even that doesn't have guarantees. Like a pacemaker for your heart, even it can stop working. But I think clinical help along with diet and possible medications could have bought them time.

People have poor lifestyles and life circumstances that lead to heart or other organ failures, but we don't place action verbs on them. We don't say "she heartattack-ed herself" or "he cancer-ed himself" or "she diabetes-ed herself." Some of those deaths are because of years of poor eating, alcohol abuse, smoking, lack of activity, etc., but we still say they died "from" or "by" or "of." We have compassion for the way their life ended before it's perceived time, and we research how to heal those organs or systems proactively and reactively. We give them grace through compassion. I don't think suicide is any different. Hearing action verbs about someone who died by suicide is like fingernails down a chalkboard for me. I always let it slide though, because it takes time for someone to understand that, if they ever do. And I'm sure many would even disagree. The longer we place blame on those dying, the longer it will take to get to proactive clinical detection and treatments.

Plus, there's safe talk. We don't want to go on giving people ideas for when life isn't going smoothly by leading them to believe they can be in control of their circumstances in such a way. Instead, we use words indicating that those that die by suicide are victims. They are casualties of a disease, a brain disease.

I recently went to a suicide prevention training course put on by the American Foundation for Suicide Prevention (AFSP). They listed the correct ways to talk about suicide like "killed themselves" and "took their life." I raised my hand and questioned this after the PowerPoint presentation-style training. I asked how that would sound in front of a kid and mentioned how saying that could be a contagion in itself. I also mentioned how the word "committed" was frowned upon and was in the not-to-use list because it insinuated the person was bad or sinful, and that these terms also placed blame and maybe even manifested anger towards the person who died. While my opinion and feedback were listened to and respected, they simply shared that this is what research found, and that "yes" we should be aware of our audience when sharing about suicide.

Days later, I am still up in arms over these terms being taught to everyone. I feel they are misguiding people. I'm wondering if I'm triggered because I know better, or it struck my heart strings. I found the whole moment eye-opening and have been pondering it since. It is interesting how much those terms made my skin crawl when reading them listed so casually on the screen. There's that chalkboard sound. I felt like my loved ones were being insulted and disrespected. I felt embarrassed to have suicide losses when I saw that on the screen. Now I'm wondering if they have it wrong or if I'm just hyper-sensitive on the subject.

I'm thinking I'm going to start saying people heart-attacked themselves when they were overweight now. I mean technically they did it to themselves right? All is fair in love and war, right? Or did they do it to themselves? Some would say, similar to suicide, that societal pressures, foods, and bad habits have "fed" and created the problem. Perhaps this approach will open people's eyes.

Am I wrong or insightfully correct? Perhaps I've not truly come to acceptance, and I've just become aware of that. But wait, if I am this upset over it, aren't I a missing subject of the research, which proves that perhaps it wasn't fully completed? It seems to me the suicide stigma was glaring right at me there on that screen during the training.

I called my great friend and Survivors of Suicide (SOS) loss co-facilitator, Jacqueline Wastal, who lost her sister to suicide nearly four years ago. She is also mere months away from being awarded a Master's in Mental Health Counseling. I just had to converse with someone who was both a survivor and studying clinically on mental health. She gasped on the phone when I told her what was on the screen as the perceived correct terminology. She too does not agree that these are acceptable terms. She said something amazing that explained why I don't like the term "killed themselves." She said murder is to kill someone, and that's bad. She's right! I couldn't initially articulate why it was bothering me so much. My mind immediately felt that they were wrongfully blaming my loved ones of murder. That's why I felt embarrassed in that room full of facilitators.

Jacqueline and I delved further into the word "killed" in our conversation. In the Bible the sixth commandment says: "You shall not murder." - Exodus 20:13 "The taking of human life is expressly forbidden. Jesus elaborates on this commandment in the Sermon on the Mount, revealing that the sin of murder begins in the heart." - Matt 5:21-22

But suicide begins in the brain, a sick brain. So, I believe in the vast majority of suicides, grace would absolutely be extended by God, because suicide is almost always not an evil act of the heart.

As Jacqueline and I moved on to the word "took," we discussed how that can insinuate wrongfulness, especially in many stages of grief like anger and resentment. "Took" could also insinuate "stolen," or a wrongful decision was made to do something once you added "life" to the end of the sentence. *Took their life.* Sprinkle in confusion and despair, and that is received horribly.

In the training, it was shared that "committed" is frowned upon because it could be tied to thinking of being incarcerated or committed to psychiatric care. These things are thought of negatively. How is that different from "killed" and "took"? No matter how you try to spin it, these phrases are accusatory and conjure up bad emotions. How did their research miss that?

I also reached out to Jill McMahon via email who wrote the forward of this book. She wrote something so powerful in response to my inquiry: "If a term feels offensive to you then it is offensive. A professional doesn't need to tell you how you feel or try to change your mind."

My reaction is proof of my point. We still have a long way to go. So, when someone says something silly or inappropriate, give them some grace. It takes time to change a culture.

It's hard to make sense of all the thoughts that go through your head when you lose someone to suicide. You never see yourself perhaps losing someone to suicide much less twice. It also makes many of us evaluate what's most important in life, and how trivial so many things are.

I was approaching forty. Many people say when you approach forty, you start to evaluate your life. I was starting to realize how unhappy my sister was, and how my dad retired well and wasn't happy either. I then realized happiness comes from the inside, and I need to do some serious work. That's what brought me to the light, a true understanding that you don't get joy and happiness out of thin air, you cultivate it inside. You get it from yourself, despite your life around you. I didn't yet know exactly what I needed to do to get it, but I had a great idea on what I needed to get rid of.

I realized there's more to life than the stress of my job. I was working for an employer for nine years at the time, and they'd compassionately supported me through both suicide losses. I learned a lot from this employer. It really was a great employer and taught me a lot from a professional standpoint, but it was also very toxic for me. I had golden handcuffs on me too. It was a very dysfunctional employment. It was a co-dependent situation.

I decided that I needed to leave this employer. It was too much of an unhealthy environment. We had people in the office crying because of the way they were spoken to. They were only interviewing and hiring men for new jobs by design. I always thought, *What the heck are you doing, Jenny? You're gonna be where your dad is at. Are you really that co-dependent on this employer? You're not even happy. You think this money is buying you happiness. You have money, but—wakeup call! —you're not happy!* That was hard to process, let me tell you, because then I started to self-judge.

Self-judging can be really debilitating, let me tell you. You start to self-judge yourself and you're thinking, *Jenny, you've really done a job on your life. You've worked for this company who hasn't really appreciated you. They've appreciated the fruits, but not the person that made the fruits. What are you doing? You need to get the heck out of here.* And that was not easy to do after nine years, right? I'd been there over a third of my professional career and nearly a quarter of my whole life. It was literally like a divorce.

I started searching in the industry. A chef shared with me that a company had come in high on price and could use my help. He gave me a business card and I called the owner. Long story short, I left that employer a year after making that life-happiness decision and almost two years after I lost my dad. I took a 20% pay cut. My checks were lower by a lot, and I was so happy. Ridding myself of the toxic environment was a weight off me. Even my sons said to me a few months after starting the new job that they didn't even know who I was anymore, because I was so pleasant and nice all the time.

Not that I was always mean or anything, but I always had this horrible job I went to everyday just for money, which I thought was supposed to make me happy. But I wasn't happy. When I realized how happy I was even making less money, I said to myself, *Well, I'm never doing that again. I'm either gonna be happy, or I'm not gonna be there.*

I stayed with that next employer for nearly five years. Well, I didn't leave there, I was fired so the owner could free up cash to buy another home. I didn't know that until eight months after I was let go, when a former employee shared that insight with me. So, another case of making someone money and helping them, but it was all unappreciated in the end. I told myself I'd never do that again, so I didn't have any regrets. In fact, later I was quite grateful I was let go. But initially, I was an emotional mess and a lot of old grief started coming back up. I felt rejected by my employer and I was wronged. Those emotions brought the suicide rejection back to the forefront.

Now what? Now I had been rejected again, and I was jobless. It helped that two large competitive companies called right away looking to hire me once they heard I was no longer with that employer. That gave me quite a bit of confidence. My husband and a close friend of mine, Angelica Sanchez, strongly encouraged me to finally start my own company. What? That was a scary idea. But I had very large companies calling to hire me, and I didn't have an employment agreement with my former employer. The timing was right, and I had a lot of support. Plus, I could support whatever I wanted with profits, and I could take care of people with whatever compassion I wanted to give. So, I did it!

But something was still missing. I needed a purpose. A bigger than just daily-life purpose. Without that, I feared I may be destined the same as my sister and Dad regarding lack of life fulfillment. My sister had a purpose (kind of), which was her daughter. I still don't know if she had a why, but I don't think so. My dad didn't know his why or purpose. He had placed it all in his job and kids. He didn't know of any other way to make an impact in the world or in his life in his mind. Life is more than just living through the motion of waking up every day, going to work and going to sleep. Wake up. Go to work. Go to sleep. Wake up. Go to work. Go to sleep. All with a little sprinkling of self-care and/or hobbies... maybe.

I was afraid after I lost Dad. I was trying to figure out if suicide was in my genes? Is this like the breast cancer gene they test for? Is there some kind of suicide gene? I don't want to die. So, I had to figure out how I wasn't going to die if this was a gene thing. I knew that meant I couldn't be like Dad by way of finding my only purpose in my job and my kids. It had to be bigger. It had to be a purpose in my heart. A purpose to help others and to give back, because, really without that, what is your soul doing?

I thought, *How am I gonna make an impact on the world right now? What am I passionate about?* I always wanted to be like my dad, and I am like him for sure, but I didn't want to be unhappy like him. What better way to honor him than to make life better than he did? That would make him proud. My dad was my everything. He was an incredible person. He was a great parent. I missed him so much, but I didn't want to be unhappy like him. I dislike saying these things about him, but I didn't want to be the Negative Nancy that he was.

I started to take a heart inventory. I literally started to evaluate my heart and say, "Okay, how is your heart going to live with meaning?" And I really wanted to do the SOS facilitation, but I didn't feel I was in a heart space yet where I had a lot to give out of my cup. A lot of that reason was, because, if I was not happy, how was I going to be a beacon of hope?

By the time my dad died, I was wearing sequins maybe three to four times a week, and then that quickly morphed into five on the weekdays and then seven days to include the weekends. I just started to create this new me. I started wearing sequins after my sister died, and I had dyed my hair red. I think I was going through an identity crisis, and now it's like an act of Congress to go back to blonde from red. It's a six-to-eight-month process, and I don't have the patience for that. So red for life it is! Between red and the sequins alone, I have a brand. Then you take my sense of humor, my passion to compassionately serve the suicide grief and risk community, and my air-headedness sometimes, and you have "JennyLand." If I'm meeting someone, new people will think, *Oh, it's the redhead with the sequins.* I walk in to meet people I'm referred to, and, oftentimes, they're waving me down before I've even identified myself. I get such good feedback on the sparkle, and I really think it brightens people's days without them even knowing it.

Shout out to my friend, James Bennar, who coined the term "JennyLand" on card nights. My crazy antics and shameless shares inspired him to give it a name.

I started to kind of move on with life as this perceived sparkle queen, though not yet sharing the meaning of the sparkle. My story. My purpose. I wanted to volunteer for SOS as a facilitator for the peer-support groups, but I was still attending them as I needed support. They were so helpful. There were a couple of people, one in particular that I met there right after my dad that I still talk to this day. She lost her husband to suicide, and we just connected. You meet a lot of people at SOS, and it puts your loss into perspective because you meet people that get it. Your thoughts are not so crazy anymore.

Like that thought that I had when I felt relief after my sister died. I felt guilty for thinking that until I learned in that group what that relief was and that it was normal to feel. I was able to put that in perspective in SOS, because I realized that other people that had suicide-watch journeys and/or drug addiction or alcoholism stories also had that same feeling. They were always so stressed out over the monitoring of the concern and trying to keep their loved one safe and alive.

After my sister's death but before my dad, I wasn't yet to the point of understanding that this was not a selfish act. Many people who lose someone to suicide or hear of somebody dying by suicide, say it's so selfish. I was still kind of in that mode, but I had come to peace with the fact that she just had all this pain and turmoil in her life and was mentally ill. I just kind of let that be, and I wanted to help other people process grief. I was working on signing up for training, but then I lost my dad.

Right before my dad died, I started doing these greeting cards, and I put a lot of stickers on them, put little message cards that pop open in them, put confetti in them and lots of love. I had given my dad one of those cards for his birthday and Christmas before he died. I'm so glad that I'd already started that hobby before he passed away. That card hobby got up to sixty to seventy cards per month at one point. I even had a custom easel made to put my sticker rolls on dispensers. It was a fun hobby for many years. I don't really do them anymore though. They were what I needed to do for those many years. Maybe one day I will get back into them. They were a great way for me to give back to people and spread some happiness. Now I sometimes hand out disco balls to people instead. Ha!

At one point I was just addicted to helping people and doing more for everyone. I wanted to be the change. One day my son called and said his high school was starting a badminton team. He asked if I wanted to coach. I thought, *Heck yeah!* I immediately called the school and was on my way to being a parent volunteer coach. That was so much fun mentoring girls. It was not just about the sport. It was so much more. Great times. I would still be doing that, but I started working for my last employer. That experience really pulled me to volunteer for SOS in time. It gave me the confidence to know I could, and I should.

There's more to life than just education, raising a family, or having a job with your final goal of retirement. Then what? Ah! We don't talk about that. We must help each other. There's more to life than money and comfort. There really is, you have to have a purpose. You must be helping, whether it is feeding people, helping to employ the homeless, coaching, mentoring, something! I always say, if you aren't giving of your time, talent/skills, and/or money, you aren't living life to its fullest. In some way, you must give back and help this world. People need it. Plus, when you teach people to help others, then they learn to help others, and then they learn to help others, etc. It's a beautiful circle of influence.

Chapter 9

How to Be a Lifeline

To this day, I vividly remember my first dream of Jacque after she passed. It felt like it really happened. That's why I believe it has touched my heart so much and has made a big impact on me. It's like a real-life memory. I was in a big SUV. It was the kind with the third row in the back, like an Expedition. I was in the third seat in back on the driver's side, so the furthest from the exit door which was behind the front passenger seat. It was dark in the cabin of the truck even though it was light outside. It's interesting that's where I was sitting, similar to the way my grief made me feel like I was left behind and feeling like I couldn't escape the darkness.

As I was just watching aimlessly out the window, I saw my sister in another similar SUV, in the same seat going the opposite direction. She too was looking out. We were almost mirror images of each other. Our eyes locked onto each other, and you could see and feel the sheer relief and excitement that we felt to see each other. We watched one another for a few seconds as our necks twisted to keep our line of sight out of the back windows. Our vehicles immediately came to a screeching stop as she and I crawled recklessly to our exit doors, hurdling over seatbacks across the cabin. We each almost fell to our knees as we jumped out of our vehicles from built up forward momentum without caution.

Like in the movies, we ran to each other with our arms open wide, almost feeling the embrace before it even happened. Our arms flailed back, because the wind was blowing hard as we seemingly ran faster than humanly possible. Our hair looked like a dog's ears as it put its head out of a moving car's window, taking in the freedom. It was like the weight of all our grief suddenly vanished. Poof! No more pain. The wind on my face in the dream felt like a thousand caresses, healing everything.

I cannot even explain the hug. It felt like a thousand years overdue. I'd been yearning heavily for that embrace for months. Finally, she was in my arms. Finally, she was safe. Finally, her absence was gone. Tears streamed down my face in overwhelming happiness and relief bundled up in one beautiful moment.

I'm sure you can imagine the moment when I woke up, only to realize it wasn't real. Yes, it wasn't real, and it wasn't a pretty day to come to terms with that. But what a great memory. Maybe I really did hug her. Maybe she came in my dreams to tell me she loved me and to remind me that it was not my fault. To give me the forgiveness I thought I didn't deserve. The forgiveness I didn't really even need, but I didn't yet understand that. I believe my sister came to me in the only way that she could. That dream did so much for me.

I went to see a psychic medium after Jacque and again after Dad. After my sister, I didn't get much from the visit, except I realized it was legit a few months later. The medium kept referencing Chris and Madi, but I didn't know anyone with those names particularly close to me. I was frustrated when I left that meeting. A few months later, the person that referred me to the medium asked me how it went. I said it was okay and briefly mentioned that Chris kept wanting me to tell Madi he loved her. On the other end of the phone there was silence. I said "Hello?" thinking I lost the call. She was tearing up in joy as she explained how she heard of the medium. Her friend lost her husband, Chris, in a tragic car accident and left behind an infant daughter, Madi. I get goosebumps every time I share this story. So crazy.

The medium had mentioned a metal medallion with a rose on it. I had no idea what he was talking about. A few months later, I knew. My sister had bought me this beautiful handmade beaded necklace and bracelet set for my birthday a few years before she died. I treasured that set after she died because she had not given me many gifts. We never really made a big deal about birthdays growing up. That's probably why I'm such a birthday junky now. I'm making up for lost time. One day, a few months after that first medium appointment, I noticed the latch on the bracelet had a dangling tiny medallion. I always knew it was there but never paid much mind to it. Guess what was on it? Yup. A rose. Goosebumps again.

Before I go on, I want to say my dad was an amazing parent and a model citizen. I am forever blessed and grateful he was my parent. I'm proud to call him my dad, and I am proud of him for the parent he was for me. But as all parents know, we are ultimately not perfect and make mistakes. Dad didn't really praise us or brag about us. He didn't tell us he was proud of us. And, I have to say, I still have a long way to go in this realm myself. While I learned the lesson of love and have redirected myself on that, I still struggle with sharing how proud I am of those closest to me. So weird. I just don't get it. I tell others about my pride in those closest to me, but not directly to the ones I am proud of. Well, I don't tell them enough. Since my dad never told me he was proud of me, he always left me with the need to try to do better and to make him notice me. It's really done some damage to me emotionally. But I always knew Dad was proud. It's so weird. I knew but never heard it. That's how I know *words matter*. Words are powerful, and even the void of them can cause damage.

Back to my story, because of these two medium visits, I went back to the medium when my dad passed. The medium kept putting his thumb on his chin in a specific position and motion. He made this face like he was trying to figure out what my dad was trying to tell him. Mind you, the medium knew nothing about my dad or our relationship, not a thing about it. He went on to say, "Your dad wants to tell you he's proud of you."

****

I just fell into tears after typing that.

****

You should have seen me at the appointment. I was a sobbing mess. Literally bawling in relief and gratitude. I kept saying, "Thank you, Dad" over and over. I didn't know what I needed. I had never even verbalized it. The most I'd done in the past was ask my dad why he couldn't just be happy with me when he would criticize me. Some parents criticize instead of encourage. They think they *are* encouraging you. Approach matters. He just didn't understand that. He was human and doing the best with what he knew. In this meeting, he gave me exactly what I needed. He always knew and didn't know how to do it differently. Here he was showing up and making up for lost time. I'm forever thankful for what he, or I should say God, gave me that day even in Dad's physical absence.

That moment changed my life. I've never looked back. My limiting beliefs were lifted. It was like the chain holding me back from being all I could be in life fell to the ground. This moment was the catalyst for my future. My life's calling. My Why, which is God. And my Purpose, which is to serve others.

I want to quickly talk about mediums and the Word. It has been shared with me that going to psychics and mediums is a no-no. I'm not sure what to think. How can what I heard from my dad be bad? It brought me to Jesus, to helping people, to writing this book, to being a better person, to gaining a better understanding of life in so many ways, and more. That single line of "He's proud of you" has brought more light to my world. I find it impossible to believe that that's bad. And if it was, I've already asked for forgiveness. I didn't ask about my future. Not once. I told the medium up front that I did not want to know about my future. I told him I wasn't there for that. So, ultimately, no one got hurt, and Jesus has forgiven me. That's where I sit on that topic.

At Dad's funeral, there was standing room only and the crowd overflowed into the lobby. Yet, he didn't call any of us or them before his final act. Actually, it later occurred to me that he had withdrawn from hanging around his friends or shooting and camping with them for months. He had intentionally alienated himself and lived like a hermit for most of the year prior to his passing. I didn't notice that until after the crisis. All the friends and family surrounding him couldn't fix his mental health. He needed to do selfcare work for himself. He needed to learn his own self-love. He couldn't receive the outpouring of love from family and friends because he didn't love himself. Many people like him don't even feel worthy of love from others.

The reason I've shared these stories is to open up the topic about prevention. I literally almost lost my own life after my sister passed. I almost lost any life purpose and drive after losing my dad. But things happened in my life to change my course. Things turned me around. I had an open heart even though it was broken. My open heart felt and saw things that were needed, and now here I am working towards making a difference in the world.

That's what we need to do for others if they are at suicide risk or have attempted suicide. They need something, even if it's small or if it lasts for a moment, to change their course and turn them around in their thoughts. Although you do want long-term results, oftentimes the help that is needed is for just that moment. A hug. A talk.

****

To know when you need to help prevent suicide, you need to know when there's a risk. You need to know the warning signs. These are listed on the NIHM site. https://www.nimh.nih.gov/health/topics/suicide-prevention

WARNING SIGNS that someone may be at immediate risk for attempting suicide include:

- Talking about wanting to die or wanting to kill themselves
- Talking about feeling empty or hopeless or having no reason to live
- Talking about feeling trapped or feeling that there are no solutions
- Feeling unbearable emotional or physical pain
- Talking about being a burden to others
- Withdrawing from family and friends
- Giving away important possessions
- Saying goodbye to friends and family
- Putting affairs in order, such as making a will
- Taking great risks that could lead to death, such as driving extremely fast
- Talking or thinking about death often

Other serious warning signs that someone may be at risk for attempting suicide include:

- Displaying extreme mood swings, suddenly changing from very sad to very calm or happy

- Planning or looking for ways to kill themselves, such as searching for lethal methods online, stockpiling pills, or buying a gun
- Talking about feeling great guilt or shame
- Using alcohol or drugs more often
- Acting anxious or agitated
- Changing eating or sleeping habits
- Showing rage or talking about seeking revenge

****

From NIMH, here are **RISK FACTORS**. https://www.nimh.nih.gov/health/topics/suicide-prevention. Suicide does not discriminate. People of all genders, ages, and ethnicities can be at risk. Suicidal behavior is complex, and there is no single cause. The main risk factors for suicide are:

- Depression, other mental disorders, or substance use disorder
- Chronic pain
- A history of suicide attempts
- Family history of a mental disorder or substance use
- Family history of suicide
- Exposure to family violence, including physical or sexual abuse
- Presence of guns or other firearms in the home
- Having recently been released from prison or jail
- Exposure, either directly or indirectly, to others' suicidal behavior, such as that of family members, peers, or celebrities

Most people who have risk factors will not attempt suicide, and it is difficult to tell who will act on suicidal thoughts. Although risk factors for suicide are important to keep in mind, someone who is showing *warning signs* of suicide may be at higher risk for danger and need immediate attention.

Stressful life events (such as the loss of a loved one, legal troubles, or financial difficulties) and interpersonal stressors (such as shame, harassment, bullying, discrimination, or relationship troubles) may contribute to suicide risk, especially when they occur along with suicide risk factors.

Family and friends are often the first to recognize the warning signs of suicide, and they can take the first step toward helping a loved one find mental health treatment. See the resources on NIMH's Find Help for Mental Illnesses page if you're not sure where to start.

****

Here are the **PREVENTION TIPS** from NIMH. https://www.nimh.nih.gov/health/topics/suicide-prevention

Here are five steps you can take to #BeThe1To help someone in emotional pain:

1. **ASK:** "Are you thinking about killing yourself?" It's not an easy question, but studies show that asking at-risk individuals if they are suicidal does not increase suicides or suicidal thoughts.
2. **KEEP THEM SAFE:** Reducing a suicidal person's access to highly lethal items or places is an important part of suicide prevention. While this is not always easy, asking if the at-risk person has a plan and removing or disabling the lethal means can make a difference.
3. **BE THERE:** Listen carefully and learn what the individual is thinking and feeling. Research suggests acknowledging and talking about suicide may reduce rather than increase suicidal thoughts.
4. **HELP THEM CONNECT:** Save the National Suicide Prevention Lifeline's (**1-800-273-TALK (8255)**) and the Crisis Text Line's number (**741741**) in your phone, so it's there when you need it. You can also help make a connection with a trusted individual

like a family member, friend, spiritual advisor, or mental health professional.

5. **STAY CONNECTED:** Staying in touch after a crisis or after being discharged from care can make a difference. Studies have shown the number of suicide deaths goes down when someone follows up with the at-risk person.

****

PREVENTION TIPS from AFSP.

What to do when someone is at risk.
If you think someone is thinking about suicide, assume you are the only one who will reach out. Here's how to talk to someone who may be struggling with their mental health.

Have an honest conversation

1. Talk to them in private
2. Listen to their story
3. Tell them you care about them
4. Ask directly if they are thinking about suicide
5. Encourage them to seek treatment or contact their doctor or therapist
6. Avoid debating the value of life, minimizing their problems, or giving advice

Assume you're the only one who will reach out

If You're Concerned About Someone. Talk in Private.
Listen to their story and let them know you care. Ask directly about suicide, calmly and without judgement. Show understanding and take their concerns seriously. Let them know their life matters to you. That one conversation could save a life.

If a Person Says They Are Thinking About Suicide. Take the Person Seriously.
Someone considering suicide is experiencing a life-threatening health crisis and may not believe they can be helped. Work with them to keep them safely away from lethal means like firearms and drugs and remind them that their suffering is temporary.

Stay with them and call the National Suicide Prevention Lifeline: 1-800-273-TALK (8255).

Be sure to follow up with them after the crisis to see how they're doing.
If You're Struggling. Don't Wait for Someone to Reach Out.
Seek mental health treatment or tell your clinician about your suicidal thinking.

Treat yourself like you would treat someone else who needs your help.

If a person says they are considering suicide

- Take the person seriously
- Stay with them
- Help them remove lethal means
- Call the National Suicide Prevention Lifeline: 1-800-273-8255

- Text TALK to 741741 to text with a trained crisis counselor from the Crisis Text Line for free, 24/7
- Escort them to mental health services or an emergency room

****

Here's what I can share from my experience. Time matters. Just delaying their thoughts can turn things around… at least for that moment in time. You can buy time in many ways. Talk to them on the phone and keep them on the phone. Maybe drive to them while you are on the phone. Go hang out with them, even if you end up doing nothing together. It may not be the most upbeat hang out time, but this isn't about you. It's all about them. They may not be up to going out, but your presence will be felt. If you feel they are a danger to themselves or you, call 911 and/or get them to the hospital right away. Don't wait.

Never assume it won't happen. Instead, always assume it will, so you can prevent it. Losing my dad to suicide was a huge awakening for me. It can happen again. It can happen to anyone. For many years after my dad died, I had this very real fear of everyone dying by suicide if they were quiet or mad at me. It mainly manifested with my husband and my boys. If Mike was in the garage for a long period of time, I would go check that he was still alive. If one of the boys was grounded, if they were mad or pouting, if they were in their room for a long time, or if they were quiet for a long time or sleeping in late, I would do a life check. They started to realize what this nervous distress habit was all about. There were even times I would do a life check to calm my anxiety, and they would say in an annoyed tone, "No, I'm not dead." But this fear was so real. I was always panicking that I was going to walk into that. It was this nervous tick for years. I was trying to get ahead of more regrets.

What I wouldn't give to go back and stay on the phone with my sister while on Fremont Street in Las Vegas. Or to have flown to her when she wouldn't come to us. What I wouldn't give to just suck it up and say "yes" to Dad helping Mike move. Or to notice he just needed company and driven over there to be with him. I'm convinced loneliness is one ingredient that can lead to a recipe for disaster. Don't leave them alone if you can prevent that. They usually don't want you around. They are miserable and don't want to involve you or they just want to suffer alone. Don't allow that. Don't ask for permission to come over. Just go so long as you believe it's safe. There are some cases in which calling 911 is necessary. You have to make that judgment call. Either way, time is of the essence. Time is not your friend, but it is theirs. Give your time to them.

That gets me to my next share. Be there. Just your mere presence can change the course. Yes, it's heavy, but that's just for that moment. While there, work on a future mental health clinical care plan. When people are in crisis, they most often do not have the mental capacity to do the leg work for clinical care. You must search for providers. Then you have to call to see who is seeing new patients. I recommend you physically drive them to their first few appointments even. They need our help seeking care. It is fascinating to me that we actually think people in mental health crises are of the mind frame to prepare their mental health care. It's so ridiculous. Health plans should have mental health concierge services to assist in mental health cases. I'm sure that would save lives.

This is also why I think we need asylums back. They would literally take you in and plan all your mental health care in one facility. They cared for you until you were considered stable to live life productively again; not until you just weren't a perceived risk to yourself or others. You weren't just on suicide watch. They rehabilitated you.

Asylums got such a bad rep, because they weren't overseen and structured enough to be successful forevermore. I won't get into the details of all of that, but they were a great thing. We need them back with good programming. People need a safe place to get proper mental health care, not a general hospital. They need a big place, like an entire facility the size of a major hospital with rooms only for mental health care patients. A big, safe place. That's an "asylum." It's such a dirty word now. Maybe we could bring them back but name them "sanctuaries." Wouldn't it be nice to say, "My loved one is at a sanctuary?"

We also need to heal our other brain, the gut. We need to get back to the basics and evaluate our guts in detail and heal them. They are the other brain that greatly affects the major brain. Our food and average diet, especially in America, is poor at best. So bad. We can do so much for our mental health with food. Natural healing from the inside-out. I could go on and on about this. There are lots of doctors out there that can do full workups and blood panels, including your stool. They can guide you on this journey. I personally see a naturopathic doctor since they have tons of hours in nutrition under their belt. You'd be amazed at how they look at blood panels and your gut.

Water. DRINK WATER. Stop consuming sodas or energy drinks and never look back. They are not good for you no matter what they tell you. Sugar is in all of them. Sugar alternatives are not fooling your gut either. Do yourself a favor and never drink another one starting today. I never had soda in the house with my kids. To this day at ages twenty-three and twenty-five, they don't drink soda. It's not their thing. It was never a staple in our home. I didn't do so well with energy drinks. I thought for a long time that they were okay. They are not. Just put water in your body all day and lots of it. The average body is 60% water, so you literally are what you drink by 60%. If you drink coffee, soda, tea and/or fruit drinks all day, that's who you are. And keep in mind most of those drinks are acidic in pH and the body/blood is meant to be a neutral pH. Give it water instead to promote this.

I am not a nutritionist, but I have self-studied this area for years. I am convinced that what we eat, and drink have profound effects on our physical and mental wellbeing. It impacts our moods, energy levels, and decision-making skills. I would highly encourage you to read up on this subject to better understand the human connection to food. There are a ton of books to choose from. You could even start with a nutritionist and/ or naturopathic doctor to guide you.

I am simply sharing my opinions with you. My opinions are based on true life experiences and educating myself through many forms of media. I've even personally made most (if not all) of the changes I mentioned. I've literally watched my face reverse in age as I changed my diet. It hugely affected my emotional well-being too for the better. I am never going back. My mental health is my responsibility. I can either choose to protect it or let it get by as best it can as I consume whatever I want and live my life without care for myself. I've noticed the amazing difference with my natural reactions and my outlooks on things since changing my diet and practicing daily gratitude. I've been my own experiment. Do your own work and you too will see great things in your life.

We should be educating children EVERY YEAR in school on nutrition and coping skills. Can you imagine what the world would be like if we were all well-educated on nutrition? I feel we should also be educating people on coping skills too. If I had the time, I would work to pass legislation to add a permanent school curriculum on coping skills and life essentials. Why wait? These are life skills that will change the world. Maybe this book can inspire someone to take on this task.

In Chapter 12, we will review ways to cope with life in detail. Below are suicide statistics so we can grasp the importance of understanding suicide risks and prevention. My point in sharing all this data is **YOU ARE NOT ALONE**. Do not feel embarrassed. Do not feel like you must hide. Do not feel ashamed of you or your loved one. Often, the person sitting right next to you has been touched by suicide themselves. Talk about it.

****

Mental illness is the cause of most suicides.

The newest report from the National Alliance on Mental Illness (NAMI) shows the scope of mental health problems in the United States and some startling facts about suicide. https://nami.org/mhstats

1 in 5 U.S. adults experience mental illness each year.
1 in 20 U.S. adults experience serious mental illness each year.
1 in 6 U.S. youth aged 6-17 experience a mental health disorder each year.
50% of all lifetime mental illness begins by age 14, and 75% by age 24.
Suicide is the 2nd leading cause of death among people aged 10-34.

You Are Not Alone

- 21% of U.S. adults experienced mental illness in 2020 (52.9 million people). This represents 1 in 5 adults.
- 5.6% of U.S. adults experienced serious mental illness in 2020 (14.2 million people). This represents 1 in 20 adults.
- 16.5% of U.S. youth aged 6-17 experienced a mental health disorder in 2016 (7.7 million people)
    - 6.7% of U.S. adults experienced a co-occurring substance use disorder and mental illness in 2020 (17 million people)
- Annual prevalence of mental illness among U.S. adults, by demographic group:
    - Non-Hispanic Asian: 13.9%
    - Non-Hispanic white: 22.6%
    - Non-Hispanic black or African American: 17.3%

    - Non-Hispanic American Indian or Alaska Native: 18.7%
    - Non-Hispanic mixed/multiracial: 35.8%
    - Non-Hispanic Native Hawaiian or Other Pacific Islander: 16.6%
    - Hispanic or Latino: 18.4%
    - Lesbian, Gay or Bisexual: 47.4%

- Annual prevalence among U.S. adults, by condition:
    - Major Depressive Episode: 8.4% (21 million people)
    - Schizophrenia: <1% (estimated 1.5 million people)
    - Bipolar Disorder: 2.8% (estimated 7 million people)
    - Anxiety Disorders: 19.1% (estimated 48 million people)
    - Posttraumatic Stress Disorder: 3.6% (estimated 9 million people)
    - Obsessive Compulsive Disorder: 1.2% (estimated 3 million people)
    - Borderline Personality Disorder: 1.4% (estimated 3.5 million people)

- Mental Health Care Matters
- 46.2% of U.S. adults with mental illness received treatment in 2020
- 64.5% of U.S. adults with serious mental illness received treatment in 2020
- 50.6% of U.S. youth aged 6-17 with a mental health disorder received treatment in 2016
- The average delay between onset of mental illness symptoms and treatment is 11 years
- Annual treatment rates among U.S. adults with any mental illness, by demographic group:
    - Male: 37.4%
    - Female: 51.2%

    - Lesbian, Gay or Bisexual: 54.3%
    - Non-Hispanic Asian: 20.8%
    - Non-Hispanic white: 51.8%
    - Non-Hispanic black or African American: 37.1%
    - Non-Hispanic mixed/multiracial: 43.0%
    - Hispanic or Latino: 35.1%

- 11% of U.S. adults with mental illness had no insurance coverage in 2020
- 11.3% of U.S. adults with serious mental illness had no insurance coverage in 2020
- 55% of U.S. counties do not have a single practicing psychiatrist
- 134 million people live in a designated Mental Health Professional Shortage Area

The Ripple Effect of Mental Illness

PERSON

- People with depression have a 40% higher risk of developing cardiovascular and metabolic diseases than the general population. People with serious mental illness are nearly twice as likely to develop these conditions.
- 32.1% of U.S. adults with mental illness also experienced a substance use disorder in 2020 (17 million individuals),
- The rate of unemployment is higher among U.S. adults who have mental illness (6.4%) compared to those who do not (5.1%),
- High school students with significant symptoms of depression are more than twice as likely to drop out compared to their peers,
- Students aged 6-17 with mental, emotional, or behavioral concerns are 3x more likely to repeat a grade.

FAMILY

- At least 8.4 million people in the U.S. provide care to an adult with a mental or emotional health issue.
- Caregivers of adults with mental or emotional health issues spend an average of 32 hours per week providing unpaid care.

COMMUNITY

- Mental illness and substance use disorders are involved in 1 out of every 8 emergency department visits by a U.S. adult (estimated 12 million visits).
- Mood disorders are the most common cause of hospitalization for all people in the U.S. under age 45 (*after excluding hospitalization relating to pregnancy and birth).*
- Across the U.S. economy, serious mental illness causes $193.2 billion in lost earnings each year.
- 20.8% of people experiencing homelessness in the U.S. have a serious mental health condition.
- 37% of adults incarcerated in the state and federal prison system have a diagnosed mental illness.
- 70% of youth in the juvenile justice system have a diagnosable mental health condition.
- 8.4% of Active Component service members in the U.S. military experienced a mental health or substance use condition in 2019.
- 15.3% of U.S. Veterans experienced a mental illness in 2019 (31.3 million people).

WORLD

- Depression and anxiety disorders cost the global economy $1 trillion in lost productivity each year.
- Depression is a leading cause of disability worldwide.

It's Okay to Talk About Suicide

- Suicide is the 2nd leading cause of death among people aged 10-34 in the U.S.
- Suicide is the 10th leading cause of death in the U.S.
- The overall suicide rate in the U.S. has increased by 35% since 1999.
- 46% of people who die by suicide had a diagnosed mental health condition.
- 90% of people who die by suicide had shown symptoms of a mental health. condition, according to interviews with family, friends, and medical professionals (*also known as psychological autopsy*).
- Lesbian, gay and bisexual youth are 4x more likely to attempt suicide than straight youth.
- 78% of people who die by suicide are male.
- Transgender adults are nearly 12x more likely to attempt suicide than the general population.
- Annual prevalence of serious thoughts of suicide, by U.S. demographic group:
    - 4.9% of all adults
    - 11.3% of young adults aged 18-25
    - 18.8% of high school students
    - 42% of LGBTQ youth
    - 52% of LGBTQ youth who identify as transgender or nonbinary

If you or someone you know is in an emergency, call The National Suicide Prevention Lifeline at 800-273-TALK (8255) or call 911 immediately.

2020 Mental Health by The Numbers
RECOGNIZING THE IMPACT

- 1 in 15 U.S adults experienced both a substance use disorder and mental illness
- 12+ million U.S adults had serious thoughts of suicide.
- 1 in 5 U.S adults report that the pandemic had a significant negative impact on their mental health.
    - 45% of those with mental illness
    - 55% of those with serious mental illness

- Among people aged 12 and older who drink alcohol, 15% report increased drinking.
- Among people aged 12 and older who use drugs, 10% report increased use.
- Among U.S. adults who received mental health services:
    - 17.7 million experienced delays or cancellations in appointments
    - 7.3 million experienced delays in getting prescriptions
    - 4.9 million were unable to access needed care

- 26.3 million U.S adults received virtual mental health services in the past year.
    - 34% of those with mental illness
    - 50% of those with serious mental illness

YOUTH & YOUNG ADULTS

- Among U.S. ADOLESCENTS (aged 12-17):
    - 1 in 6 experienced a major depressive episode (MDE)
    - 3 million had serious thoughts of suicide
    - 31% increase in mental health-related emergency department visits

- Among U.S. YOUNG ADULTS (aged 18-25):
  - 1 in 3 experienced a mental illness
  - 1 in 10 experienced a serious mental illness
  - 3.8 million had serious thoughts of suicide

- 1 in 5 young people report that the pandemic had a significant negative impact on their mental health.
  - 18% of adolescents
  - 23% of young adults
  - Nearly ½ of young people with mental health concerns report a significant negative impact

- 1 in 10 people under age 18 experience a mental health condition following a COVID-19 diagnosis.
- Increased use of alcohol among those who drink:
  - 15% of adolescents
  - 18% of young adults

- Increased use of drugs among those who use:
  - 15% of adolescents
  - 19% of young adults
  - Mental Illness and The Criminal Justice System

CRIMINAL JUSTICE SYSTEM

- About 2 million times each year, people with serious mental illness are booked into jails.
- About 2 in 5 people who are incarcerated have a history of mental illness (37% in state and federal prisons and 44% held in local jails).
- 66% of women in prison reported having a history of mental illness, almost twice the percentage of men in prison.

- Nearly one in four people shot and killed by police officers between 2015 and 2020 had a mental health condition.
- Suicide is the leading cause of death for people held in local jails.
- An estimated 4,000 people with serious mental illness are held in solitary confinement inside U.S. prisons.

COMMUNITIES

- 70% of youth in the juvenile justice system have a diagnosable mental health condition.
- Youth in detention are 10 times more likely to suffer from psychosis than youth in the community.
- About 50,000 veterans are held in local jails — 55% report experiencing a mental illness.
- Among incarcerated people with a mental health condition, non-white individuals are more likely to go to solitary confinement, be injured, and stay longer in jail.

ACCESS TO CARE

- About 3 in 5 people (63%) with a history of mental illness do not receive mental health treatment while incarcerated in state and federal prisons.
- Less than half of people (45%) with a history of mental illness receive mental health treatment while held in local jails.
- People who have health care coverage upon release from incarceration are more likely to engage in services that reduce recidivism.

Last updated: Feb. 2022

****

The stats are from https://psychcentral.com/blog/startling-facts-about-suicide-and-mental-illness#1

- 50 percent of all lifetime mental illness begins by age 14, and 75% by age 24.
- At least 8.4 million people in the U.S. provide care to an adult with a mental or emotional health issue.
- Only 43.3 percent of U.S. adults with mental illness received treatment in 2018.
- 50.6% of U.S. youth aged 6-17 with a mental health disorder received treatment in 2016.
- 60% of U.S. counties do not have a single practicing psychiatrist.
- 46% of people who die by suicide had a diagnosed mental health condition.
- 90% of people who die by suicide had shown symptoms of a mental health condition, according to interviews with family, friends, and medical professionals (*also known as psychological autopsy*).
- Suicide is the #2 cause of death among people aged 10 – 34 in the U.S.
- The overall suicide rate in the U.S. has increased by 31% since 2001.
- 11.3% of U.S. adults with mental illness had no insurance coverage in 2018.
- Across the U.S. economy, serious mental illness causes $193.2 billion in lost earnings each year.
- Depression is the leading cause of disability worldwide.

****

These are the statistics from The American Foundation for Suicide Prevention. https://afsp.org/suicide-statistics/

- Suicide is the 12th leading cause of death in the US
- In 2020, 45,979 Americans died by suicide
- In 2020, there were an estimated 1.20M suicide attempts
- The age-adjusted suicide rate in 2020 was 13.48 per 100,000 individuals.
- The rate of suicide is highest in middle-aged white men.
- In 2020, men died by suicide 3.88x more than women.
- On average, there are 130 suicides per day.
- White males accounted for 69.68% of suicide deaths in 2020.
- In 2020, firearms accounted for 52.83% of all suicide deaths.
- 93% of adults surveyed in the U.S. think suicide can be prevented.

Chapter 10

Traveling Together Through Grief

I've experienced several suicides from as far back as the age of sixteen. My first suicide was a friend, Danny, in 1991. I wasn't close to him, but it affected me in a big way. That's another reason how I know that the grief from suicide can reach far and wide. Then my friend, Rick, passed in 1992. So, in high school, I experienced two suicide losses. It was sad and shocking. I was living my own life, trying to get home before the streetlights turned off, while others were in the depths of despair. I just couldn't make sense of it. Back then, it was a very hush-hush taboo. There wasn't a community or a school outreach. At least, not that I was aware of.

I lost my 2nd cousin, Dim-Ray Stokka, on March 27, 2004, so just a few years before Jacque. I was pretty confused when Dim-Ray passed away. My younger cousins were good friends with her, and they said she was always so delightful and upbeat. She wrote letters and even included funeral instructions. That was so hard for me to process, but sometimes I wish I had a letter like that. She was only eighteen when she passed away. I couldn't wrap my head around what could be so bad at the age of eighteen. This was after Gwynnie died, so everything was compared to that despair at the time. It made everything seem so trivial. Her despair had not been trivial though as she lost her life.

Then I lost my sister on January 1, 2008, and my dad on January 3, 2012.

My son's girlfriend, Lena Way, passed away on June 15, 2017. She was only twenty years old. She struggled with some recent life let-downs and mental health. She was a Christian and a member of a church. She had an amazing support system and was surrounded by great people. I remember that night my son asked me to let her in at the front door. I went to the door but didn't see her or her car. She was in crisis, but we didn't know it. When I told him I couldn't find her, he said she went home. All seemed normal. She passed away within thirty minutes. Still seems like a dream. She was an amazing singer. Her voice was like an angel, and she had a smile that would light up the room.

Another friend of mine passed away in October 2020. He was so much fun and willing to help anyone. He was such a gentle soul and very generous. He struggled with mental health. I remember several years prior he called me asking for help and we talked. He was thinking about driving his truck on the freeway over 120 MPH and ramming it into an overpass concrete pillar. He wanted to make it look like an accident so life insurance would pay his family. Can you imagine being this sad? It physically makes my heart hurt typing this. He called to talk it over and stop himself. He struggled with suicide for many years, and many people knew it. We still couldn't save him.

By age forty-five, I'd experienced one drowning, one murder, and seven suicides. Real tragedies. Mind-boggling tragedies. These deaths were not from cancer or old age. These were all surprise deaths. Because of the shock and devastation after the death, I rate massive heart attacks right up there with surprise deaths. They take you on a roller-coaster ride of grief.

Suicide is a real epidemic. It affects all ages, races, cultures, genders, societal sects, etc. It doesn't matter who you or your family are and how great they may seem; suicide can touch your family. So can mental health problems, which is at the root of most suicides. Someone dies by suicide every eleven minutes. Suicide is in the top ten causes of death in the United States, yet we still don't treat mental health with the gravity and seriousness that we do with a heart attack patient. There is an unequal treatment of mental health in our health care system, which leads to unnecessary death. If you have a sick heart, the hospital will go through all sorts of hoops to treat you now regardless of insurance you may or may not have. If you have a sick brain, they'll be sure to watch you now until your current risk passes, but the outpatient treatment for long term mental health is often dependent on your insurance.

Everyone is struggling in a different space. Their reality is real to them. You can't tell people they are overreacting and think it'll be fine. You can't just tell them to grow up, get over it, or question their grief or despair. They are not you. Just talk to them. Merely talking can buy them time. And many times, time is all you need to get them past their current thoughts or emotional turmoil.

I like to use a commonly referred to analogy with mental illness; LUV them. Listen. Understand. Validate. A doctor at a convention was sharing a story about LUV. A patient diagnosed with schizophrenia was in his colleague's office, and the patient thought he was Jesus. The doctor walked into the office and said, "So, I heard you are a carpenter." Immediately the patient finally felt heard, understood, and validated, all in one statement. The doctor then proceeded to tell him he needed a bookshelf built. He gave the patient all the materials. He said it was the worst constructed bookshelf, but he reached his patient.

He approached his patients with LUV, so he could truly reach them and gain their trust. He met them where they were, and not where he forced them to be. They then followed the treatment plans. He had many people in remission from schizophrenia for years with this tool.

Most of us would want to look at that person and remind or convince them that they are obviously not Jesus. But think about that. They are not well. Their brain is sick. If you fight their thoughts, they will not trust you. They truly believe their thoughts. No matter how outlandish and outside of reality they are, those thoughts are very real to them. You can use LUV in everything you do. Everyone wants to be heard. Everyone wants to be understood… even if that means that you meet them with understanding and recognize what they need. Everyone wants to be validated. These are ways to let them know that they are heard and understood.

I had a friend call me earlier in 2021 concerned about his son who was in his early 20s. He was scared about his mental health and not sure what to do. His son was in the hospital because he was a suicide risk, and he didn't know what to do upon his son's release. His son was experiencing extreme paranoia and displaying peculiar behavior. Mind you, this was a child who was close to finishing college. He was a successful kid by societal standards and heading in the right direction. Over the past year or so up to this call, he had erratic, unexplainable behavior. But being away at school allowed for the behavior to be undetected. His parents didn't realize how bad it was or that he was on a downward slope to a mental health crisis if he continued without professional treatment. Of course, I recommended a care facility that could focus on his long-term recovery and teach coping skills, rather than referring them to a typical clinical approach, which simply released you once you were no longer at risk.

If a person wants out of the hospital, they could suddenly change their behavior to indicate their symptoms have cleared and that they are coping. They often do what is needed to get out, which leads to them masking the continued crisis. Life demands it because of their responsibilities from their school, job or kids can lead a person to lose focus on their mental health.

My call with my friend was a short one, maybe 5-10 minutes as he seemed to be in a hurry. Upon ending our call, I told him there was one thing I felt he must know so he could connect with his son rather than losing touch with him. I shared the story about LUV. I received a call out of the blue early January 2022. He wanted to thank me for the LUV analogy. He said that LUV was such a crucial piece of information, which allowed him to have compassion and understanding during the process of healing his son. His son is now back on track with life with a diagnosis and proper medication.

When it comes to families and grief, you can also use LUV and you should at every opportunity you get. I believe the three key ingredients for a grieving family are (1) get help, (2) talk, and (3) understand, and in this order.

Professional help is so crucial. It's nearly impossible to be there for each other while you too are grieving the same loss. A clinician can guide you through the process successfully. Don't skip this step. Many people do for different reasons, but eventually that grief will creep up on you in days, months or even years later. I've seen it so many times in my SOS groups. Support groups are a great tool as well. They should not be used in place of counseling though. They should be coupled with counseling. You may even need to see a psychiatrist for medications to help you. I had to temporarily take an antidepressant for over a year after both my sister and my dad passed away.

Talk amongst your family members. It's okay to cry together. It's okay to be vulnerable with each other. Being vulnerable is a great model for children so they know it's okay to be sad. Talking opens the lines of communication. If someone is having moments of despair, they will be more likely to open up to another family member. Make a pact to tell each other if someone gets that low in their grief. Maybe have a sign. Perhaps you could have a cup that you flip upside down in the living room to signal that you are at your low point. No words needed. Then you could all sit down for a meal together, go for a walk, play cards, watch a movie, and there is so much more you can do. If the cup is flipped, it's family time. Tell each other when you are missing your loved one. Share funny and memorable moments. Be a family more than you ever were before.

Understand that everyone is in their own grief, so they cannot necessarily be the end-all, be-all person to watch over you. This is why counseling and group support is so important. You need to get it out. You have to talk about it. Talking about how you feel, no matter how big or small, will help you heal. Understanding that you each need help is important. Understand that each of you is grieving too. Understanding that no one's grief is more important than another is so important. This will seem odd to hear, but a mother and a friend's grief are just as important, one does not beat out the other in significance. Each person processes grief differently. The grief isn't about the relationship to the person lost. The grief is about the person who is actively grieving. They may be more emotionally in touch with themselves. They may have never dealt with grief before. They may have a tough time grieving so they hold everything in, most often leading to difficulties later.

Years after my sister died, I remember one time one of my siblings yelled at me on the phone about not even noticing they were suicidal and really struggling with the loss of Jacque. I was beside myself. I defended myself and reminded that sibling that I was dealing with the same grief. I mentioned that it was not fair to hold me accountable for their grief when I could barely handle my own. We were both grieving. This is why counseling is key. Your family members cannot be your keeper when they too are grieving. They are navigating the same despair. My sibling and I didn't talk for over a year after that. Well, that sibling wouldn't speak to me. I let it be as I was still grieving when they said that to me. I couldn't take on that heap of guilt. It was guilt that wasn't mine to take on anyhow.

I did nothing wrong. If my sibling had gone to a counselor and shared that overwhelming feeling, our relationship would have turned out differently.

There's this thing where siblings and children get left behind or get lost in the shuffle of grief. I can't tell you how many times someone, especially at the funeral, would ask how my dad and mom were. Like WTF? Was I a ghost here? My mind envisioned me looking behind me like they had to be talking to someone else. What about me?! I grew up with her. I spent far more actual time with her than my parents did. I was much closer to her than they were, but somehow, I was chopped liver. My grief seemed trivial in comparison. This happens often with children as people ask the child how the other parent is doing. Then the siblings and children tend to shrink into a shell and feel left behind or unnoticed. Their grief, which is perceived as seemingly insignificant, makes them feel that other people's perceptions place a different value on their grief than what they feel.

Everyone matters in grief. Siblings, children, friends, significant others, neighbors. EVERYONE. Not just the societal hierarchy focal point. Grief isn't about the relationship. It's about the impact that loss has on the person grieving. Maybe the person that died was your neighbor's only confidant. Maybe the one who was lost was a child's only parental figure in their life, despite not being blood related. It's the impact from the loss of love, not about the bloodline of the relationship. I've seen friends devastated from losses, sometimes it is felt more than losing a parent or sibling. You just never know, so ask everyone how they are doing and how you can help them.

Grief is a lifelong journey. Grief is the price of love, and you never stop loving your loved one. You just learn to live life with it. You learn to bear with that hole in your heart.

I was in the car the other day and I just started crying. I just wanted to talk to my dad right then about all the shit that was going on in the world. He had been so freaking smart when it came to worldly things and politics, and I just wanted to talk to him. I was thinking to myself, *This is crazy that he's gone. I still can't believe this happened.* That didn't mean I was not healing or healed. It didn't mean I took a step back. It didn't mean I was a mess. It meant that I was human. It meant that I was healthy. It meant that I loved my dad, that I still love my dad, and will always love my dad. We can keep loving them and we will. Grief just looks different as we learn how to not be able to actively love them anymore.

Chapter 11

Finding My True Hope

Remember that carnival ride called Gravitron? It was this ride that looked like a flying-saucer-type spaceship. When you walk in, you pick a spot on the wall. There are these sliding pieces you lay on with a backwards slant. As you are laying back, the ride starts to spin so much that your back slides and raises you up, lifting your feet from the ground. When you get off the ride, you are so dizzy, and you're lucky if you don't vomit. I wasn't one of the lucky ones. I feel like my life has been like that. I'm always pulling forward, but I feel dizzy and fall backwards. It's like a double pull. My life seemed to go backwards so many times even though it was forging ahead. The same is true of my faith. It came backwards… later in life. I always believed in *a* God of sorts, but I was never subjected to the teachings of God, Jesus, and evil in my family. I never knew the Word. We didn't even own a Bible. I was very naive in my "faith," like it was something I needed so I didn't go to hell, but I really didn't get it.

My limited belief of something in my teens and younger 20s was very vague, even to me. I thought there was a higher power of sorts, and He was supposed to work everything out to perfection and shield us from pain. You can imagine my surprise through my life journey. I didn't even describe the last two departures from long-time jobs, which had been very traumatic. I would compare them both to an ugly divorce. Three tragic deaths, one divorce, and two messy employment changes. I thought there was no way there was a God. No way a God would allow this much pain in my heart, with sick brains that saw no other way out other than death or allowing innocent children to die painfully. I was mad at any higher power out there. It was His fault. I was mad at Him, and no way was I going to give Him my heart after what He had done to it.

That was my ignorant self before dedicating my life to Christ. Fast forward to 2020, I learned a lot of coping skills and I strongly believed that we lived in a great universe with energy I could easily draw from. 2020, what many people would call the worst year in the history of mankind, was the best year of my life. When the lockdowns started in March 2020, I was so upset that the gyms were closed. Mental health needs human connection and a moving, sweating body, among other things. And those two things together are magic! My mental health was slipping fast. I had been practicing yoga and lifting at the gym consistently for two years prior, and then it was just gone. I was livid about that. Meanwhile, I could easily go get McDonalds, the amazing by-product poison called "fast food." It was so backwards.

I noticed that a few yoga instructors I followed were posting pictures of group hiking and yoga. I didn't know the instructors well, but I followed them in case of events or retreats they may post. I wanted to be out with people, so I messaged on one of the posts asking how I could be a part of their group. My friend, Hanan Palz, immediately said that I should just come on the next excursion and that she would include me in the invitations. That was the beginning of finding my "why." I always thought my "why" was my lost family members, but boy was I wrong.

I started hiking, practicing yoga, paddle boarding and PRAYING with the women. They were ALL lifelong Christians. I was so blessed to find them. I got to see the wonderful lives they lived, strong and long-time marriages they had, beautiful homes they lived in, hearts of gold they shared, successful children they reared, and I heard about Jesus ALL THE TIME. They could barely have a conversation without talking about Jesus.

I would talk about how "the universe is good," or "the energy is flowing to me/us." Many times, I would hear little nudges from my new sister, Hanan, that it was actually Jesus. They would always pray and, of course, I would join. How could I say no? But the amazing thing was I felt the Holy Spirit in my heart in those prayers. I really started to realize that Jesus had always been there. He had always carried me through the path to my greatness. I couldn't be great without my experiences. I slowly started to come to this realization.

One day, Hanan said to me, "You know you've always been doing work for Jesus; you just didn't know it." That hit home! I was starting to realize that. The most beautiful thing about that year was because of what they all taught me. They taught me the love of Jesus. That He gave us free will. That there was evil in this world. They answered my question when I asked why Jesus allowed all this tragedy and pain. They helped me understand the workings of evil, that God had a plan that we didn't understand. That those who accept Jesus will have an everlasting life. This life on Earth was only a small part of our journey. Jesus had a plan for my life and molded me to be ready, and most of all, JESUS LOVED ME. I was saved by His blood. He gave His life to wash away my sins, and He was giving me an everlasting life of peace and joy.

The highlight of my week is going to Bible study with these wonderful women of God. My faith is unfaltering. I learn more of the Word all the time. My Bible study sisters teach me so much. They taught me Jesus' gift of forgiveness. We are forgiven for all our sins. That knowledge alone has really allowed me to forgive myself. Self-forgiveness has transformed my life. Once I forgave myself, nothing could hold me back from being the amazing human that I am and will be. I was made in the image of God and am loved by Him. I'm just in awe over His grace. Knowing He loves me and now I love me, I can not only love others, but I am able to extend grace to everyone. I can understand that others have life stressors too. The way people act or treat others is a mere expression of what's going on in their hearts and lives. All I can do is feel sympathy for them and share Jesus through my actions and words. What if they just lost someone to suicide? What if they are struggling with guilt of some sort? What if they just had a home fire? What if they lost their job? What if they don't have faith? For example, sometimes when a cashier or teller is rude or completely dry, I think about what must be going on in their life to regard others in such a manner. I simply ask Jesus to help them cope or overcome whatever is ailing or affecting them. This is what a heart of love must do.

Growing up, my siblings and I were great friends with a family who lived directly across the street from us. They had two girls and a boy as well. Michele Orabuena was a year and a grade older than me, and her sister was the same age and grade as Jacque. Jacque and I were really close to the girls. My brother knew their brother, but they weren't close. Their brother was the middle child in their family. We had so much fun with those girls. I will forever treasure the stories we have together, and we can still laugh about them. They would always talk about Jesus. Michele taught me about Jesus. They were a strong family unit with good values. I always loved the feeling I had when in their home. It gave me a sense of peace or maybe that was because the home was filled with Jesus. I'm now convinced Jesus put them in my life to prepare me for what was to come.

When Gwynnie died, Michele talked to me again about Jesus at the funeral. She made sure I did not blame Jesus. While it may not have worked, I believe it did reinforce the Holy Spirit that was always there, unbeknownst to me. Then when Jacque died, Michele reached out again about Jesus, and she brought it up at the funeral. She knew I wasn't a believer in my mind yet, but she was always discipling my heart. When my dad died, she encouraged me to trust in Jesus and to put my faith in Him. She shared that

He was always there for me to comfort me and that we couldn't understand His ways. Mind you, we grew apart after childhood. They moved away and we only saw each other at school. After school, we only really saw each other on social media. It always touched my heart that although we grew apart and never saw each other, they always came to the funerals like any supportive neighbors would. It meant so much to me. And now, the encouragement of faith from Michele makes sense. When I gave my life to Jesus, it was easy, because I immediately thought of Michele and her family. They were good people. People of faith. Strong faith. Good Christians.

Since finding Lord God, I'm at peace about Gwynnie, Jacque, and my dad. They are now at rest and enjoying everlasting life. They're in a place where they don't care about any of this. They are not sad. I just have so much solace and comfort in that. I don't like living without them here. I still desperately miss them, but I am happy they are home.

I recently lost my good friend to murder. April Jorgic was my maid-of-honor in my wedding. She passed away on October 29, 2020. She was only forty and had nine-year-old twins, who she adored and lived for. She had been a wonderful woman, never caught without her hair done, and makeup on complete with lip gloss. Never. Ever. LOL! She taught me how to put on false eyelashes and took me to my first makeup makeover appointment. She was also a model Christian who made a big impact on me. Actually, she was an inspiration as I gave my life to Jesus. She was so happy for me. I love and miss her. Her family was just beside themselves. I'm still struggling to process it, but I have this sense of peace about where she went. It's because I have God in my heart. Her family is also Christian, and they also have found an abundance of solace in Him.

Isn't it interesting how when something bad happens to us, we often ask, "God, why are you doing this to me?" But when good stuff happens, we aren't so quick to think of God or thank him. Now, I always say, "God, you are amazing. You are so good to me." I even get tears in my eyes sometimes at the amazingness of it. It's the little miracles every day. Sometimes, it's the event, sometimes it's timing, and sometimes it's the feeling. I'm always saying, "God, you are so, so good to me. I mean, when you're good, you're good!" Anytime something goes well, even the smallest little thing, I thank Him.

What about bad things? Those are of the enemy. You have to back up and ask, "Would Jesus do something bad to you?" No. Life is a result of free will, decisions made by us, and others. The devil is of this world, the devil was cast out into this world, and he's here. He's convincing us to make bad decisions for one reason or another. Maybe we watched too much TV. We have crime, we have drugs, we have alcohol, we have addiction, and all these things are from the enemy. We also have emotions we fail to control like anger, jealousy, lust, and many more. Instead of letting the enemy in, we need to say to ourselves, "Stop, Satan. You're not allowed in my life. I rebuke you." Instead, many of us say, "God, why are you doing this to me?" We need to reframe our thoughts about the bad things that happen in life.

Maybe Gwynnie would be alive had my sister decided to take Gwynnie out of that environment full of risk. What prompted her to delay that decision or second guess her worry? Do you think that was God or Satan? I think it's easy to pick. What if my sister had stuck with a counseling program or quit drinking? Would she still be alive? Probably, but bad decisions were made. Also, a broken health care system that made her wait and, in my opinion, led to her ultimate demise. Who broke that system? God or Satan? Easy. Satan. What if my dad had taken his prescriptions? What made him decide not to take care of himself? God or Satan? Easy again.

I still struggle processing evil too. I am always questioning my Bible study sisters in my infant journey of the Word, and they are amazing disciples. But let me share a little miracle with you of something that Jesus does all the time to me. At our weekly Bible studies, I always hand out these little message cards at the end. At a recent Bible study, I was questioning why God allowed the trafficking of innocent children. I was just so broken up about it. My sisters encouraged me to remember it was the work of the devil, not God. They reminded me God prevails in the end and that we do not have the capacity to understand His plan. I have to stay strong in my faith. At the end of study, I passed out the cards like I always did. I randomly picked a card, and Jesus gave me a message at just the right time: "For God so loved the world that he gave his one and only Son, that whoever believes in him shall not perish but have eternal life." John 3:16.

Bam! It was a reminder to me of what God did for us. He gave His only son for our sins. Imagine giving up your child for someone else's decision to sin, so they may have an everlasting life. If you don't know the torturous way in which Jesus died, read *The Case for Christ* by Lee Strobel, or watch the movie, *The Passion of the Christ.* I can't read a certain passage in the book or watch that movie again. They both make me cry. I don't understand it all, but God is my Savior. He made this world, and I am in His image. That's what I know.

I'll never forget this one day, and I'll preface this with the fact that it's not the only time it's happened. A few years ago, I didn't know how I was going to make payroll. One of the biggest pains of running a business can be payroll timing versus when receivables come in. I was thinking, *Oh my gosh, it's over, this is the end of the road.* I got really weird about payroll, a little too overboard about it. I was serious about paying people on time. I processed payroll and was leaving for Bible study. As I walked out the door, I looked up and audibly said, "You know what, Jesus, this is in your hands. I'm going to Bible study, I'm just gonna leave it in your hands. I don't know what's gonna happen, but you've always taken care of me before. Do your work." I came home just a few hours later, and there was $60,000 in checks in the mailbox. I walked into the house with tears in my eyes and overwhelmed with gratitude. I said to Him aloud, "I leave the house for two hours and ask you to deliver, and you send 60 grand to my mailbox. You rock!" Prayer and leaving it all in His hands is powerful.

I always run late to everything. They've done studies on that, and they say that most people that run late are actually optimistic, because they always think they have time to do something more. They don't mean to be late. It's not from disrespect. They genuinely believe they can fit more in, and those personalities tend to be very optimistic in general. Since finding Jesus though, time has been moving slower. I swear it has! Oftentimes, I'll be caught up and look at the clock realizing I need to leave, only to find it's 10-20 minutes earlier than I thought it would be. How is it only that time? I swear I've done more than 10-20 minutes' worth of stuff. I'm just killing it on timing because He is giving me more time. It's crazy, I know, but I'm convinced. It happens so much. I always say, "Thank you, Jesus. I'm gonna be on time."

My son called me this morning and said, "You know what, Mom, when you're good…" And I finished for him, "You're good, and there's nothing you can do about it." That is a saying we have in our house. It ultimately means that "You ROCK!" It's self-bragging with some "umph!" because we all should do it! Now, I add to our saying, "I'm telling you; God is good."

My boys originally questioned my dedication to Jesus even though they applauded me. I feel guilt and celebration all in one crumpled ball about sharing my faith with them. I felt guilt that I did the same to them that had happened to me growing up, not teaching them about Jesus. I did nothing, so they too didn't have a sense of the evil in the world. But I celebrated because they encouraged me. We had a Bible… somewhere, but it was still pristinely new. So, they also can't believe there's a higher power with all the worldly nonsense out there. All I can do is start now by leading with faith by example. That's more than I received, so I am already doing better. And you know what? Now, a year later, when I say, "God is good," they too say, "God is good" in return. That's progress!

God has done miraculous things in my life in just the last three years alone, and no doubt He is the creator. I tell people all the time, if you're not sure whether Jesus lives, I say again, you should read Lee Strobel's book AND maybe his other book, *The Case for the Creator* as well. I read them both so I could better defend my faith when attacked. Also, READ THE BIBLE. The Word will call to you and open your heart. This world has conditioned us to turn to evil and believe in nothing. We need to turn that around.

The Case for Christ is a really good book. Lee Strobel was an investigative journalist and had a law degree from Yale. So, he was all about gathering the facts and having all the information for your case. He was married with a toddler child, and his wife was pregnant. His wife suddenly started going to church and believing in Jesus. He was an atheist. He asked her how she could be a part of a cult. He said she wasn't the same woman he married. Their marriage was in trouble over this. He decided to prove to her it was a sham. He started interviewing and meeting with theologians. The theologians he interviewed were true experts in their field, many had written several books already. He even traveled for the interviews. Literally every chapter, everyone testified that "Jesus is real. Jesus is real. Jesus is real." By the end of the book, I felt very confident in defending my faith. Lee is now a man of strong faith. Here was a guy hell-bent to prove that his wife's faith was ridiculous. Now he's a believer. A die-hard atheist turned American Christian author.

I asked my oldest son if he would just read to page eighty in *The Case for the Creator*. He said, "Oh my gosh, Mom. Are you serious?" Cody was working for me that day, so I told him he was on the clock. So, I was paying him to read. How could he say no to an employer assignment? After a serious eye roll, he agreed to read it. Those eighty pages talk about how the proof they used for evolution has been disproved, yet they still teach it. If their proof has been disproved, it shouldn't be taught. It goes over all the details of how the date they use has been disproven. They don't teach the Bible in school. There's no tangible proof for creation, and there's no tangible proof for evolution. So why teach one and not the other?

I have this bust figurine of Jesus. It's a little painted, porcelain figurine. I remember that thing as far back as when I was five years old. I think it might have been made by or belonged to my grandma on my dad's side. When Dad died, one of the first things on my mind was, *Where is that little Jesus figurine?* It was worth nothing and meant the world to me. It now sits on my kitchen windowsill, so I see it every day. It's one of the altars in my house. It's my Jesus altar. I was thinking the other day, *I almost feel like this is my dad's way of saying that he always believed in God.* That figurine never went away. It was always in our home as a part of the decor. We always had Jesus.

The Book of John in the Bible is often referred to as the Book of Love. So, the name, John, my father's name, is known to mean Love. I think my grandma somehow left a generational footprint for the future of her family. It definitely made an impression on me. Here I've found God despite all things I've been subjected to. I've endured them because of God. All this time I was being guided by love and continue to be guided by love to this day. I'll never forget that epiphany I had at my very first Bible study. I don't think it was a coincidence that was the first chapter we studied. God sent me that message at just the right time. He's always been there for me. Always.

God is Good.

****

"Let all that you do be done in love."
1 Corinthians 16:14

LOVE

Bonus Narrative 3

God's Plan for Sparkles

I met Jenny or "Sparkles" as I affectionately call her when she took one of my yoga classes at Mountainside. I often have new people come into my class and while I make an effort to meet them, if they don't come back, I rarely remember them. Jenny was different. She walked in wearing the most flamboyant yoga pants along with a glittery top and sandals. I could tell she had a tenacious spirit by how hard she worked. Eventually she became a regular and we chatted often after class. She regularly made comments on the serendipity of various events as "the universe" was watching out for her but I would gently question her about how the universe was orchestrating these events and comment that perhaps it was God's watchful eye on her and not the galaxies made of rock that were in charge.

She eventually told me her story and how she had the resilience to pull herself out of a deep depression and intentionally decide that she was going to live her best life as a tribute to her sister, father, and niece. Finally, her tenacious spirit, outrageous outfits and even her red hair all made sense.

You see, God did have a plan for Jenny's life, and He needed her to stand out in a sea of ordinary to be that beacon of light to help others struggling with suicide and loss, to help them find their way home to Him so that they too could live out His plans for their lives as well.

After a few years of the Lord's continued wooing and in the midst of a pandemic, she finally came to accept Jesus as her Lord and Savior. The prayers of her mother's friend as well as countless others along the way were answered and I was honored to witness Jenny declare her love for Jesus as she was baptized at Dream City Church in September 2020.

Jenny has seemingly a limitless amount of energy with which she runs her own business, volunteers at many places, studies God's word, celebrates with friends, works out and takes the time to make personal birthday and thank you cards for everyone she knows. It is impossible to be in Jenny's presence and not feel joyous. She exudes happiness and always leaves you with a little card reminding you of a reason to be grateful or of a Bible verse that speaks directly to your heart.

I am so thankful to count her as my friend. I am certain that her book will help countless others find their joy and hope and I look forward to seeing all the places God takes her to be His hands and feet to the brokenhearted. Jenny epitomizes Matthew 5:4, "Blessed *are* those who mourn, for they shall be comforted."

Hanan Palz

Chapter 12

Your Joy Toolbox

Grief is not a train you get on and get off. It is a lifetime train ride. It's your choice if you ride on a jalopy train or a luxury train. Choose wisely.

The jalopy train is all over the place. You have no idea where it's going. It's a rough ride. It makes you dizzy with all the bumps and jerks. The amenities are horrible. Tiny little seats you can't get comfortable in. The seat springs hurt your butt. You want to get up, but if you do, you'll only get dizzy again. No fresh air, all the windows are screwed shut, keeping you from the outside world. The windows have an old tint, so they are streaky, and everything outside looks blurry. The tint keeps the coach dimly lit and the lighting is constantly flickering at the rhythm of the bumps. You can't really enjoy any of the views during the ride. You spend your time in one of two places: sitting in your seat uncomfortably or throwing up in the bathroom. You find yourself in the bathroom a lot, but oddly unable to recover and get yourself together. You simply wobble back to your seat and await the next vomit episode. You spend most of your time thinking about how to settle yourself and how to stop yourself from throwing up again. All the while, vomit is sitting at the top of your throat as you keep swallowing to stop the inevitable. It's horrible. Just horrible.

The luxury train is beautiful. It's the opposite of the jalopy in comfort. It's spacious. There's plenty of fresh air coming through some of the open windows, and the freshly cleaned windows allow you to enjoy all the wonders going by. The lighting makes everyone, and everything look so beautiful; like they are lit from the inside out. It has a tiny little bathroom though. It has just enough room to do your business. You only go to the bathroom when you need to use it, but you *must* use the bathroom. We all have to use the restroom, and what I mean by this is vomit AKA grieve. That's the thing about grief, you need to grieve. You can either hold it in and wait for it to deal with you later with its surprise timing, or you can deal with it regularly with purpose on your own time.

It really is a simple choice. The grief isn't simple or easy, but the choice is. Do you want to be on the jalopy or the luxury train? The answer is obvious. How do you go on that luxury ride? You grieve on purpose with purpose. You must be intentional with your grief so you can find joy in moments, days, and years. Let yourself grieve, don't hold it in. Suffering is created by resisting grief. If you encourage yourself to grieve, your suffering is nonexistent. You will still miss your loved ones. You will still want to love them here and now in this life on Earth. Your heart will still ache for them. But you won't be suffering from resisting. This is a journey we must navigate. We shouldn't stop and stay in a moment forever. We must forge ahead whether we like it or not. It can feel like you are being forced to do so, feeling like life shorted you, or you can choose to forge ahead with purpose, knowing life is not within our control. This train ride can apply to a variety of griefs: divorce, bankruptcy, lawsuits, trouble with the law, children in tough times, and much, much more.

I could have easily named this book *Suicide to Sequins*, but I named it *Suicide and Sequins*. That was an intentional word choice. "To"' leads one to believe you transition away from grief to joy, but you transition *through* and *with* it. You aren't defined by your grief or what happened to you, but it is instrumental in shaping you into the person you are now and will be in the future. Here you are reading this book, most likely due to the grief you are navigating, and you are looking to improve how you live with it and bear it. You start by acknowledging and accepting the grief. You are already forced to live with it but embrace it for what it is. Grieve. Let yourself grieve.

You can still work to live in joy. You can't just sit around waiting for it though. If you do that, you'll never find it. Joy is self-made. It's love and compassion, constantly oozing out of you. You have to give yourself joy by, first, allowing yourself to feel joy. By loving yourself enough to allow yourself to love and enjoy things in life. Try this mirror exercise. Write this on a card in your own handwriting and read this to yourself while looking yourself in the eye. Crying is okay, and you may want to plan for it.

I love you, [insert your name here].

I really love you.

I forgive you, [insert your name here].

You deserve all the wonders of life.

You will have all the wonders of life.

I love you so much.

You are amazing.

The United States Declaration of Independence states, "We hold these truths to be self-evident, that all men are created equal, that they are endowed by their Creator with certain unalienable Rights, that among these are Life, Liberty and the pursuit of Happiness." The pursuit of happiness; it's always been an intended life destination. Another word for happiness is joy. Both can be defined as a state of being happy. I like to differentiate the two. I've been happy hundreds of times over the years, maybe even thousands, but I was not living in joy. The difference is despite bad times or bad days, I still love myself and life and enjoy life. You don't have to be happy all the time to live in joy. But you do have to be in a state of happiness to live in joy.

A primary key to live in joy is by giving back. We should always be giving to the community by using whatever is at your disposal, whether it comes from your wealth, the dedication of your time or talent, whatever you have to give. I currently volunteer my time to facilitate peer-support groups for grief two nights per week. I volunteer with two different organizations to reach more people. My long-term goals are always about giving to others. I wrote this book to help others. I'm thousands of my own dollars into this book with no idea if I will ever recoup that amount. But I am not doing it to make a profit. I am doing this to help others. I used my riches, time, and expertise to give back with this book. In time, I will create a non-profit organization to PROACTIVELY help those at suicide risk as well. I will get on the front end of suicide to avoid the grief of it. We need a non-clinical way to reach those at suicide risk. Sure, it's risky and hard work, but we need it. People at suicide risk should have a safe place/space to go to get support, no matter their insurance. I'm doing all of this while running a large cleaning company, being an active member in a large networking group, and being a wife and mom.

I'm sharing these things to give you some ideas, and to rid you of any excuses of not having enough time. We all have time. We just need to allot it to the right things. Watch less TV. Be on social media less. Waste less time on things that have no meaningful return. How can you use your life experience to give back? Really think about that and take action. Call non-profits, churches or organizations that serve the community and ask if they need volunteers. Meet with a life coach for ideas. Do something. If you are not giving yourself to your community in some way, you aren't doing life right. Imagine a world if every person on Earth volunteered to help the community. It would be a more beautiful place for sure. Gandhi said, "The best way to find yourself is to lose yourself in the service of others." We can change the world one kind act after another.

I want to share this miracle from God with you. I started a commercial cleaning company in 2018. The original colors I chose were purple and a water blue. I started the company so last minute that I didn't have the time to dedicate to branding. About one year into my business, I decided to go through the process of rebranding. This is no easy task. The owner of the branding company mentioned I should change my colors to purple and teal. I was immediately opposed to it, because I would have to change uniform shirts and everything. Plus, I liked the calming effect of the blue. Because of his persistent urging to change from blue to teal, I reluctantly gave in to the professional. Fast-forward to rebranding everything with the new logo, colors, and tag lines, one day I was shopping for some suicide awareness attire, and it occurred to me that their colors were also purple and teal! What?! A year after that epiphany, I was chatting with my accountant, Youssef Khalaf, about how to best give money from the company to organizations that support the suicide community. He asked me why don't I start my own non-profit? That's when I decided to start my own. So now I have company colors that will tie right into my passion and thus my non-profit organization. God is so amazing in his work.

God calls us to love, serve and live in joy. How will you serve? How will you live in joy? How will you love others and yourself? Start today! Here's a list of ways to help you. Remember, this is a journey, not a sprint. It's a work-in-progress journey from day to day. What you do this month may look entirely different from the same month next year. The first 11 Joy Gems are in the order of my priority. After that, nothing is in order. It's a hodgepodge of things I've personally done, friends of mine have done or I've learned about. Take some time to review these often, because your needs and desires change over the months and years. Reading this list once is just not enough.

Joy Gems

1. Read the Bible
   - Be with God every day.
   - Sometimes I just randomly open the Bible and start reading. It always speaks to me. Always. The Word is the most powerful reading you'll ever experience.

2. Pray
   - Pray for what you need and want. Ask God for what you need and want. He provides.
   - Pray for others and the world.

3. Praise and Gratitude
   - Praise Jesus for everything you see, taste, touch, smell, and feel. It's all because of Him.
   - Daily gratitude is a crucial practice for joy. Do you think all these other writers, speakers, and coaches are talking about gratitude because it's a cool word? Heck no! They are talking about it because IT WORKS. Why not try it? There must be some solace and peace in it if we are all recommending it and doing it ourselves. My youngest son, Brady, gets annoyed with me sometimes. He will be complaining about something, and I'll say something that starts with "Well at least it's not…" I just naturally realize how much worse it could have been. I immediately am thankful for what it is. I wasn't like that five years ago. My long-time gratitude practice has become the very nature of myself. It's transformed my life.
   - Being happy with what you have is an amazing catalyst for a life of abundance.

4. Mindfulness and Meditation
    - Where are you living? Are you living in the past, the present or the future? It's easy to tell. How do you feel? Sadness, guilt, regret, anger, hate, bitterness, and resentment indicate you are living in the past. Stress, worry, fear, and anxiety indicate you are living in the future. The solution to these feelings is to live in the present. The past is gone and cannot be changed, so why relive it over and over in our heads? The future is not within our control. Focus on the now. The way to do this is through meditation. That word scares so many. You don't have to sit forever. You can do it anywhere and anytime for any amount of time you choose. You don't have to make it complicated. There's a ton of apps to help you too. I used to use the Muse app and headband. There are simpler apps without a headband like Calm, Headspace, Insight Timer and more.
    - Don't let your restless mind race away with your thoughts when they are completely out of your control. Choose your thoughts. Acknowledge the bad thoughts and change them or reframe them to good thoughts. Instead of thinking, *I can't believe this happened. Why did this happen to me?* Try thinking, *I can do this. God would not have given me this to handle if I couldn't bear it.* Or I'll give you an even deeper, personal example. Instead of thinking, *My Dad hurt me by not telling me he loved me. Now I am constantly working to have people like me.* I now say, *My Dad loved me and showed me in his actions. I choose to exemplify him and tell people verbally. I'm glad I learned that lesson. Thank you, Dad.* With that reframing, I am open to acceptance and forgiveness.

- Among many other benefits, meditation has been proven to reduce cortisol levels, lower blood pressure and improve the immune response. Bonuses!
- Watch this video: https://youtu.be/bAbQUO9x_8g

5. Breathe
    - Your breath is a powerful force.
    - There are lots of breathwork exercises. Learn a few that you like and use them.
    - My favorites are the belly breathing exercises. Belly breathing sends a signal that everything's okay to your body through your vagus nerve. The vagus nerve is one of the longest nerves in your body and is intimately involved within the microbiome-gut-brain connection. You can access and use this bodily tool to your benefit whenever you want.

6. Forgive Yourself and Others
    - Through self-forgiveness, we find self-love.
    - Moving forward is hard to do when you still harbor ill feelings about yourself or others. You don't have to be okay with what was done, but you should accept it and let go. Afterall, it's in the past so you can't change it. It is what it is, now move on. A lot of the path to forgiveness is in acceptance. The acceptance of what is and what cannot be changed. Don't let your mind race away with replays that will never have real life results.
    - Forgiveness is a great way to live your life with love. Love is all we need to fix the world.

7. Nourish Your Body
    - Drink 8 ounces of water every morning.

- Drink plenty of water throughout your day. Coffee, tea, and soda are not water alternatives. Actually, if you drink any of those, you'll need to increase your water intake.
- Take vitamins including lots of omegas.
- Eat as natural as you can, avoiding fast food, packaged foods, and processed foods.
- Shop the outside ring of the store.
- Cook at home as often as you can.
- See a doctor for treatment of any ailments or illnesses.
- See a nutritionist. They can help teach you the best way to eat for your body and lifestyle.
- Research the GAPS diet. Gut and Psychology Syndrome (GAP Syndrome or GAPS) is a condition establishing a connection between the functions of the digestive system and the brain. Studies have shown it can heal autoimmune disorders, many neurological diseases, and all chronic digestive disorders.
- Your body is what you eat literally, so be good to it.

8. Sleep
    - Get 7-8 hours of sleep every night.
    - Use blue light readers at night. Or put a blue light screen protector on your phone.

9. Move Your Body
    - Stretch. Seriously start your day with a long full body stretch before you even get out of bed.
    - Work out. Move your body to a sweat. Build muscle through weight lifting.
    - Practice yoga. This is a great way to combine mindfulness and movement together.
    - Run.
    - Take a daily walk.

- Hike.
- Ride your bike.
- Play some frisbee golf. Did you know there's courses out there? Yup! Fun game.
- Get a personal trainer.

10. Be in Nature
    - Walk barefoot on the ground, on grass or sand to connect with the divine energy.
    - Wear less sunblock to soak up the vitamin D. Of course, you should always consult your doctor before making this decision.
    - Leave your sunglasses at home.
    - Pick yourself some flowers.
    - Sit in the silence with nature and enjoy.

11. Talk About It
    - Call someone and chat.
    - See a counselor. This is a great way to create self-love and process/eliminate limiting beliefs.
    - See a psychiatrist for any medications you may need.
    - Go to a support group (talking with other people who understand is powerful).

12. Create Your Vision, Mission, Values and Deal-Breakers
    - These will be your guiding lights.
    - When you're not sure what to do or life seems off track, revisit them.
    - Keep them posted where you can see them each day.
    - There are a lot of resources online to help you through this process and explain what each one is and what its purpose is.
    - This is not just for business.

- Here's mine:
  - Mission
    - Make the world a better place

  - Motto
    - Do the right thing and live by the golden rule

  - Values
    - God and love
    - Gratitude, always see the bright side, positive focus leads to a happy life
    - Be you
    - You come first
    - Dream big and live abundantly
    - Be mindful
    - Spread kindness and love
    - Have fun
    - Unicorns are real
    - Sequins everyday

  - Deal-Breakers
    - Negativity
    - Drama
    - Rude/disrespectful
    - Lies/stealing
    - Self-absorbed/narcissistic
    - Runs with the wrong crowd
    - Unreliable
    - Cheater
    - Abusive
    - Judgmental/racist/bully/superiority complex

13. Love
    - Live your life guided by love.
    - Love is that feeling of inner peace and just knowing it's right.
    - If it's not in line with love, you don't need it or shouldn't do it.

14. Spend Less Time with Toxic People
    - You can't be a better person if you don't change who you are surrounded by.
    - Rid yourself of the regular time that you spend with toxic people. Don't chat with them as much.
    - Are they always bitching and complaining? Do you need that in your life?
    - Read the book *Who's in Your Room* by Ivan Misner

15. Break Bad Habits
    - Stop smoking.
    - Stop drinking.
    - Stop yelling.
    - Stop losing your temper in traffic.
    - Stop freaking out over little things or things that ultimately don't matter.
    - Need help with these things? Go to a good hypnotherapist.

16. Hypnotherapy

This is a phenomenal way to rid yourself of limiting beliefs so you can reach your true potential. Believe me, we all have limiting beliefs.

Hypnotherapy isn't how the movies portray it. You are aware of what's happening. If done right, the therapist takes your brain to a theta state (google to learn more) and helps train your subconscious to do what you want it to do.

- A really good therapist will even send you home with a recording to listen to every night.

17. Tapping Therapy
    - A great book to read about this is *The Tapping Solution* by Nick Ortner.
    - In simplistic terms, you tap the meridians on your body with your fingertips. It works! I've heard tremendous things on it.
    - Paraphrased from The Tapping Solution website:
        - Tapping, also known as EFT (Emotional Freedom Technique), is a powerful holistic healing technique that has been proven to effectively resolve a range of issues, including stress, anxiety, phobias, emotional disorders, chronic pain, weight control, and limiting beliefs—just to name a few.
        - Tapping is based on the combination of Ancient Chinese acupressure and modern psychology. The practice consists of tapping with your fingertips on specific meridian points while focusing on negative emotions or physical sensations. Doing this helps calm the nervous system, rewire the brain to respond in healthier ways, and restore the body's balance of energy.
        - In fact, it's EFT's ability to access the amygdala, the part of your brain that initiates your body's negative reaction to fear, your "fight or flight" response, that makes it so powerful.

    - My source: https://www.thetappingsolution.com/blog/what-is-tapping/

18. Listen to Sermons
    - They always have amazing messages.
    - A few of my favorite pastors to listen to are Jack Hibbs at Real Life TV, Gary Hamrick at Cornerstone Chapel, and all the pastors at Dream City Church.

19. Use Manifestation Programs
    - The Instant Switch.
    - Manifestation Magic.
    - 15-Minute Manifestation.
    - The Happiness Code.

20. Watch/Listen to Motivational Speakers
    - A few well-known speakers are Tony Robbins and Simon Sinek.
    - A few of my favorites are Dr. Joe Dispenze, Brian Tracy, and Greg Braden.
    -

21. Read Positive Affirmations
    - Manifest your life with your words and thoughts.
    - Read affirmations out loud each morning. Pick 1-5 that resonate with you now and read each one 5 times in a row with conviction.
    - Get rid of limiting words like "can't," "scared," "limitations," etc.
    - I could write a whole chapter on this. Your thoughts resonate and speak to every cell in your body, so you are what you think. Choose your thoughts and words wisely.

22. Set an Intention
    - This is purposely stating what you intend to accomplish or feel through your actions.
    - It helps you set the mood and vibe for your brain.

- They allow you to center and focus on things you want to achieve.
- It's a day-to-day practice to live more mindfully.
- My intentions usually sound something like these:
    - Today I am going to focus on things that must get done and not get sidetracked.
    - Right now, I am going to focus on me only and tune everything else out.
    - Today I am going to give more people grace and understanding. (This usually happens when I find myself frustrated with others.)

23. Speak Positive
    - Remember, you are talking to every cell in your body.
    - Maybe you don't know how. That's okay. Just copy someone else.
    - When you do something great, say to yourself audibly, "You rock!"
    - Literally say to yourself audibly things like "You are awesome, Jenny!" "You rock, Jenny." Use your name. Make it very personal.
    - Accept yourself as you are today.

24. Smile
    - Seriously, stop right now and smile. Even if it's a forced smile. Do it. Hold for 5 seconds. Isn't that amazing? That short-lived smile stirred up emotion without your conscious effort.

25. Stand Up Straight
    - Shoulders up and back.
    - Hard to do? See a chiropractor.

26. Sparkle and Spruce Up Your Wardrobe
    - Invest in some sequin and glitter attire.
    - Add lots of color!
    - For men, throw some more color into your lives. You can start with colorful underwear or socks.

27. Do The Victory Dance
    - Jump up and down with your arms up in a V-formation with a smile.
    - This will seriously increase your endorphins. Try it now.

28. Visualize Your Future Down to Every Detail
    - Literally write it down.
    - Revisit it often and visualize it again.

29. Make a Vision Board
    - Host a vision board party.
    - You can do more than one vision board.

30. Be Kind
    - I cannot stress this enough. Even when it doesn't seem someone deserves kindness, give it.
    - This helps you too!

31. Pay It Forward
    - Pay for the order behind you in the drive through, or 2 or 3 orders back.
    - Pay for dinner for a table near you, or 2 or 3 dinners.
    - Never tip less than $10 or set your own limit.
    - Tip the amount of the bill.
    - Remember to do these things anonymously.

32. Be a Positive Note Bandit
    - We had this "Positive Note Bandit" in my neighborhood that would leave handwritten sticky notes or printed squares on my car. I would get so excited to get them. I think they moved because I haven't received one in a long time. Maybe I need to become the new bandit.
    - Hand out positive messages wherever you can.
    - I'm always giving out the Thoughtful Pop-Open Cards. You can buy them at live-inspired.com.

33. Greeting Cards
    - Cards are such a lost art. No one sends cards in the mail anymore.
    - I spent 10 years with a greeting card hobby. I would cover the entire front of the envelope with colorful stickers and stamps, put confetti in the card, and a Thoughtful Pop-Open Card. They were loved by everyone.
    - You don't have to get this involved. Just send someone a greeting card for no reason at all or for their birthday. There's a high likelihood it may be the only birthday card they get in the mail.

34. Collect Positive Notes and Cards
    - Keep all the messages you receive.
    - Put them in a book.
    - Be sure to read them from time to time.
    - I have many of mine posted throughout my car.

35. Hug Someone
    - Wait for 3 breaths with your significant other. It could be weird with just anyone. LOL!
    - Really wrap your arms into the embrace. No halvsies.

36. Be Intimate with Your Partner
    - Physical touch is so healing.
    - Making love releases oxytocin which in turn increases endorphins and is a great stress reliever.
    - Even making out relieves stress. You don't always need to go to home base.

37. Get Up Earlier
    - Getting up earlier allows you to take it easy as you prepare for the day. No rushing.
    - It allows you to get more done.
    - It allows you to have time for yourself.
    - It allows you to be early.

38. Make Your Bed
    - This is a habit of starting your day with good intentions.
    - Get a nice center pillow with a message that speaks to you.

39. Go to Church
    - There's always an amazing message to take in and learn. You can and should apply these messages daily.
    - The message is my favorite part of church.

40. Splurge
    - Splurging on yourself is a form of self-care. You should not feel guilty.
    - When you spend money, spend it thinking of the experience versus gaining tangible things.
    - You can also save big on things. This can also give you joy.

41. Declutter
    - Get rid of things you haven't used in over a year. Donate it—give back.

- Organize your cabinets or closet.
- Organize your home. We hold a lot of the emotions of our past in our clutter.

42. Redecorate and Reorganize
    - You can do a room at a time as a project to keep you busy.
    - Maybe you only redecorate your walls.
    - Your furniture.
    - Move your bed.
    - Move decor around including shelving decor.

43. Journal
    - You don't need to write a ton of stuff. You can, but even a few words can be helpful.
    - Get a journal and pen that you like. Maybe get some colored pens, washi tape or stickers.
    - Learn calligraphy.
    -

44. Write
    - Write your story!

45. Color
    - There are amazing coloring books out there.
    - You could color them, frame them, and send them as gifts.
    - Maybe even get the profane words one and send them as gag gifts to your siblings or friends.

46. Draw
    - Anything. Even doodling is helpful. It brings you to the now. It's a mindfulness exercise.

47. Paint
    - Maybe a tree trunk in your backyard or a mural on a backyard wall.
    - My friend, Tamara, paints rocks and leaves them out and about for people to find. She also paints rocks for her personal hideaway garden. It's awesome.
    - You can even paint your walls.

48. Break Things
    - Yup, there's places you can pay to throw glass and porcelain dishes.

49. Listen to Music
    - Create different playlists on your phone or in your music streaming app.
    - I have one to get me going, one to relax, one to praise God, one for music my hubby likes, and more.

50. Sing and Dance
    - Take voice and/or dance lessons.
    - Learn to read music. Seriously, I joined a choir and realized I would be better if I could read music.
    - Join a choir.
    - Go out on the town with your friends to a dance club to let it all out.
    - Go to a cowboy bar with a dance floor.

51. Drumming Therapy
    - Drumming Therapy is a method of utilizing the power of rhythm and sound for the purpose of healing. Group drumming breaks down social barriers, while promoting freedom of expression, non-verbal communication, unity,

and cooperation. Studies have shown that repetitive drumming changes brain wave activity, inducing a state of calm and focused awareness.
- Yup, that loud drumming can be therapeutic! It's vibrational therapy.
- Nikola Tesla said, "If you want to find the secrets to the Universe, think in terms of energy, frequency and vibration."
- Drumming healing circles.
- Cardio drumming.

52. Cry
    - Seriously let it all out.
    - Let go of your ego.
    - Having a hard time crying? Watch a sad movie that relates to what you need to cry about.
    -

53. Emotions
    - Choose your emotions when poor ones present themselves.
    - If you get angry, turn it into something else.
    - Our reactions are choices.

54. Be With Other People
    - We are meant to congregate with others.
    - If you don't have many friends or family, join a church. They usually have groups to join too.

55. Give Yourself and Others Grace
    - Don't be so quick to judge. Remember, people most often do the best they can with their life at that moment.
    - Don't be so quick to anger. Anger affects every cell in your body. It literally lowers your immune system. Suffice to

say, it's not good for you. So, when you get angry, all you do is hurt yourself. Learn to control your anger response with grace and compassion for others.

56. Take a Nap
    - My other passion.

57. Time
    - Use it wisely.
    - Prioritize.
    - Create to-do lists.
    - Create time blocks for yourself for projects.
    - Pay others to do things for you.

58. Me-Time
    - Yes, this is a thing that needs its own bullet.
    - Be protective of your "me time."
    - It's not selfish. It's necessary.
    - You need a full cup to fill others.

59. Clean
    - Cleaning your home can be very healing. It clears up stagnant energy. It makes your home look visually pleasing. All these things combined just make you feel good.
    - It also doubles as exercise.

60. Cook
    - Stew or soup.
    - Crockpot or Instapot fun.
    - Dessert.
    - A traditional family meal.

61. Bake
    - Bake a cake and decorate it.
    - Bake snacks for your pet(s).
    - Make a homemade pizza.

62. Get a Pet
    - They provide unconditional love at your fingertips.
    - Adopt a senior or older pet and avoid the puppy phase. Lots of dogs need to be rehomed.
    - Get some fish (gaze at them daily).
    - Snuggle with your pet.
    - Take your dog for a walk.
    - Give your dog or cat a bath. (My cat LOVED baths.)

63. Read a Book
    - Escape to another world.
    - Improve yourself.
    - Learn a new trade or talent.
    - Learn about the past.
    - Learn more about someone you admire.

64. Listen to a Podcast
    - This is a great pastime to do while driving.
    - Ted X Talks are great too.

65. Take a Bubble Bath or a Long, Hot Shower
    - Add some rose or lavender petals to your bath to relax.
    - Add some scented soap for bubbles.
    - Add some citrus peels to your hot shower floor to pep you up.
    - Play some music to amp you up or relax.
    - Sing!

66. Cold Plunge
    - Cold plunges have shown to relieve muscle aches, assist in weight loss, reduce inflammation, boost energy, treat pain and help manage nervous disorders and depression.
    - They can also induce endorphin release and stimulate blood flow.
    - People with type one or two diabetes or cardiovascular disease should avoid cold plunges as cold therapy can constrict blood vessels.
    - Consult with your doctor before trying cold plunges to make sure they are a safe option for you.
    - It is important that you practice cold plunging safely as it can cause hypothermia when not done correctly.

67. Aromatherapy
    - Essential oils are a lost art it seems. They can be used very strategically on your grief journey.
    - Put in a diffuser.
    - Add them to your bath or shower.
    - Mix them into your lotions.
    - Please learn about the oils first. Not all oils are best for the above applications.

68. Crystals
    - Learn about crystals and how they can help the energy in your space.
    - Maybe even seek an expert to come to your house and help you with recommendations. Adriana Lopez, an Energy Healer and Wellness Coach, came to my home and sat in each room to assess its needs. I then placed the recommended crystals in each room of my home. Even my bathroom!

69. Travel Water Spritzes
    - Travel with small bottles of spritzes to pep and calm you.
    - Rose water is shown to relax the central nervous system.
    - Lavender water can also calm your central nervous system and help you sleep.
    - Smelling great is never a bad thing.
    - Crystal infused water in your car to bring back the energy or get rid of bad energy.

70. EMF
    - EMF's are electric and magnetic fields.
    - Try to lessen your harmful EMF frequencies and radiation.
    - We are constantly being exposed to EMF and radiation through Wi-Fi, electronics and more. There are tricks and technologies that can assist you in reducing your exposure like orgonite and orgonite pyramid. They too have crystals in them. They come in a variety of designs; some are shaped like pucks so they can be placed near a router, and others are designed as decorative pyramids.
    - I also use a USB EMF home protection tool.

71. Seven Chakra Balance, Parasite Cord Cutting
    - Parasite Cord Cutting is like when you are still thinking of your ex or someone you don't want to think of, and you don't want to.
    - Find a referred energy reader.
    - I personally have used Daniel Teague of Vega Star Healings.com. He's an International Medical Medium & Distance Energy Healer. His main purpose is to bring relief to energy sensitive people by identifying energy anomalies within a person's energy field and resolving the anomalies. His secondary purpose is to identify negative

energy anomalies in the energy field of a location, vehicle, pet and resolve the anomalies.
- Sounds foreign to many, but I have some amazing stories.

72. Create One or More Altars Throughout Your Home
    - I have five of them. One in my kitchen with avocado plants reminding me of what I can create through God, the Jesus bust figurine from my dad, a "love" snow globe, fresh flowers, crystals and an orgonite pyramid. I have another altar in my bedroom with a unicorn light, a sequin lamp, "peace" and "love" wood decorations, a unicorn snow globe, a rainbow snow globe, a yoga frog, some crystals and an orgonite pyramid. I have another small one in my guest bathroom with some sparkly knick knacks and a Bible verse; 1 Corinthians 16:14. Two more altars are in both spare bedrooms with some more unique and cool things. I also use shelving decor as mini altars; we should all do that.

73. Add a Fountain
    - Water sounds in the background are very soothing.
    - You can go big or small.
    - Be mindful if it has a battery or if it's electric, depending on where you want to place it. You wouldn't want an electric one for a center table.
    - You could even do one on your patio.

74. Volunteer to Help Others
    - At your church.
    - At local non-profits.
    - At local soup kitchens.
    - At hospices for those who have no family.

75. Delegate
    - Stop trying to do it all.
    - Give up power and watch the freedom it gives you.

76. Play a Sport
    - Softball.
    - Volleyball.
    - Badminton.
    - Pickleball.
    - Tennis.
    - Golf.
    - Swimming.

77. Go to a Spa Appointment
    - A good wash, blow and style.
    - A massage.
    - A mani/pedi.
    - Botox or filler.

78. Start a New Hobby
    - Hobbies help us grow, socialize, beat boredom and recharge.
    - Collect stamps, coins, marbles.
    - Take up welding and make some custom costume jewelry.
    - Blog.
    - Origami.
    - Garden.
    - Camp.
    - Bird watch.
    - Quilt.
    - There's a lot more of these throughout these Joy Gems.

79. Needlecraft
    - Crochet a scarf.
    - Knit a blanket.
    - Embroider your name on your pillowcase.
    - Cross stitch a pillowcase.
    - Cross stitch some flowers and frame them.

80. Photography
    - Invest in a good camera.
    - Take pictures of flowers up close.
    - Take pictures of dogs.
    - Take pictures of random things no one takes pictures of.

81. Go on a Long Drive
    - Stop at all the historical markers.
    - Have a lunch destination.

82. Go to a Public Place Even If You Are Alone
    - Go to a movie.
    - Go to dinner.
    - Doing things alone is good for you.

83. Go to a Retreat

    - Yoga retreats.
    - Men or women's church retreats.
    - Retreats for discovering more about yourself or self-development.

84. Go to a Convention
    - A gardening convention.
    - A cosmetology convention.
    - A wedding convention.

   - A trade convention.
   - A yoga convention.
   - An RV convention.

85. Go on a Staycation
    - Book an Airbnb just a city away.
    - Stay in a hotel you've always wanted to try.
    - Look for destinations online and choose one of those.

86. Go on a Cruise
    - On a local lake.
    - On a theme cruise like the 80s.
    - On a destination cruise like an Alaskan cruise.

87. Travel
    - Take that trip you've always wanted.
    - Visit a place on the other side of the globe.
    - Create a list of places you want to go to and check them off the list as you visit them.

88. Learn a New Language
    - There are great apps for this.
    - You can play in your car as you drive.
    - You can do this as an investment towards one of your bucket list destinations.
    -

89. Learn to Play an Instrument
    - If you already know how to play an instrument, start playing.
    - Try an unusual instrument like a harp or xylophone.
    - Or any instrument at all.

90. Say "YES" to More Things
    - This is your "yes life" approach.
    - When a friend asks if you want to go to a book club and maybe you really don't want to, say "yes!"
    - Say "yes" to open more doors.

91. Go to a Museum
    - The city museum.
    - A traveling exhibit show.
    - Maybe visit all the local museums over a period of time.

92. Go to the Zoo
    - Feed the animals.
    - Being around animals is so soothing for the soul.
    - It allows you to connect with nature.

93. Go to an Entertainment Playground
    - By that I mean a fair, a carnival, or a circus!

94. Watch a Movie
    - A good comedy never hurt anybody.
    - Maybe watch a sappy movie to get the waterworks going.

95. Fasting
    - From food.
    - From technology.
    - From social media.
    - From the news.

96. Jump on a Trampoline
    - Seriously, be a kid.
    - Quit taking yourself so seriously.

97. Shop Online but Don't Buy Anything
    - Just browse to your heart's content.
    - Maybe create a wish list to save for and splurge later.

98. Host and/or Plan an Event
    - Host a big dinner for no reason at your house.
    - Have a card night or giant Jenga night at your house.

99. Look for a Pen Pal Online and Write Them a Letter
    - You could even learn a new language in this endeavor.
    - Pick a pen pal from one of your bucket list destinations.

100. Buy Yourself Flowers
    - They don't have to come from someone else. If you like flowers, just buy them.
    - Sign up for an automatic monthly delivery of flowers. Let them surprise you with custom arrangements and day of the month. Then you have this pleasant surprise coming every month.

101. Play With Some Play-Doh
    - This is a great way to fidget and create all at once.
    - You can make cool things for your altars too.

102. Garden
    - To your heart's desire.
    - An aquarium garden.
    - A Zen garden.
    - A produce garden.

103. Raise Chickens for Your Own Eggs
    - You'll have those cute little furry creatures to enjoy.
    - This is a great way to stay healthy too.

104. Put Makeup On

- This can get so creative.
- Get some new lashes.
- Try new colors.
- Go big and throw in some glitter.

105. Be Okay with Rejection

- Someone's rejection is not a reflection of your worth.
- A lot of us (A LOT) have rejection scars that have us always questioning our worth and basing on what others think. Stop doing that to yourself.

106. Trust Your Gut

- This can get you into the right opportunities and out of the wrong situations.
- Remember that "yes" life but trust your gut when it gives you the creeps.
- Fear of the unknown is different from the creeps.

107. Rewrite a Bad Dream

- If you have a bad dream that's bugging you, rewrite it to a better ending to clear it up in your mind.
- Write it with a pen and paper, because your handwriting will do that work subconsciously for you.

108. Focus on Your Strengths

- Our society is so focused on short-comings and where we can get better. But what if you simply harness and do great things with what you are good at?
- We all have weaknesses. Maybe not all weaknesses need to be focused on.

109. Look at Old Photos
    - Create a book of memories.

110. Squeeze a Stress Ball
    - Many of us fidget with our hands and don't even realize it.
    - A stress ball or any fidget-type toy can be handy and soothing.

111. Save Funny Videos in a YouTube List and Watch Them
    - Here's a couple of my favorites to get you started
    - https://youtu.be/MA11NlkIREA
    - https://youtu.be/MBAObRbq66A
    - https://youtu.be/gWfaQUccxgE
    - https://youtu.be/69UlVQpYwUE

****

I would be lying to you if I said, "I'm all good now." I'm never all good. Rather, I live harmoniously with my grief. I allow it to happen. I sit and ponder it at times. I'm still learning every day.

For example, as I was driving the other day, it had been 22, 14 and 10 years since my tragic losses that I've shared in great detail with you throughout this book. I suddenly teared up and went into a moment of utter shock thinking, *How in the heck did this crap actually happen?* Suddenly, I had a moment full of thoughts like, *Holy crap. This is real. How can this be?* It almost lacks any reasonable explanation or understanding. The reason I'm sharing this with you is, so you understand we have to learn to live *through* and *with* our grief. We can't have an end goal that the grief pain will all be over one day. If we fight our grief and resist it, we will just have a harder journey on that jalopy train. It won't be a longer ride, because we all have the same length of the journey… which is for life. I had that moment, and then I chose to get back on the luxury train. Our suffering is because we resist. If we accept what has happened and live with it while living in joy, we end our suffering. I had my moment of tears, allowed it to happen, accepted it, and moved forward. I didn't stay in that moment. I didn't get stuck.

Yes, you will still have sad moments and hard times in life, but with the work you put in towards a life of joy, you will work through those moments and phases easier. You will have a clear vision of what your life will be, so it will be near impossible to throw you so off track that you end up on the jalopy train. You may have periods when you spend more time in the little bathroom on the luxury train, but you will be living life in the luxury of joy.

Don't live in resentment towards life for what it dealt you. Holding that grudge will get you nowhere. You will only hurt yourself emotionally. Those emotions are representations of you resisting the truth of the situation and your emotions. Resistance creates suffering. Don't look at life as wronging you, instead figure out what you can learn and take from it.

I challenge you to pick 11 of the 111 Joy Gems and wholeheartedly start them. Implement them today. If one isn't doing much, simply exchange it for another. Pick 6 you feel comfortable implementing and 5 that make you nervous. Grab a piece of paper or your journal and write out the 11 you picked. Start. Them. Today.

Your past is not your destiny. So don't stay stuck in it. Your past will be a beautiful catalyst or catapult to your future. You must work to get there though. You must mindfully and purposefully accept your past and move towards your future. You do it the same as you process grief; one moment at a time, one hour at a time, one day at a time, one week, one month, one year, etc. Grief can be tedious at times, but with the right frame of mind, you can live with it in a wonderful way. The fact that you are reading this book tells me you are already on your way to a healthier you and a more peaceful grief journey. You know there is hope, and you have hope. Trust in that hope.

****

"Now faith is the substance of things hoped for, the evidence of things not seen." - Hebrews 11:1

HOPE

Jenny has experienced many, tragic losses that have taken her on this journey. She uses these tragedies and the heartache that came with them to give back to the community, bring awareness to mental health and suicide, and to live a positive and inspiring life despite such life trauma. It is doable. Sometimes it's one hour at a time, sometimes one day at a time or more, but you can still live a joyous life.

Jenny is passionate about helping others learn to cope with the trauma of suicide loss and the grief that comes with it as well as learn to come to peace with suicide loss. Her hope is she can ease the pain of the journey for others by sharing what she's learned and how she's come to process her grief. She wants to additionally help readers that perhaps are in a suicide prevention journey with the prevention tips she's shared, so perhaps they may never experience suicide loss. While this book may be focused primarily on suicide and alcohol abuse, she's hopeful she will save a child's life by additionally educating readers on swim lessons...something she learned too late.

She also shares ways to cope with life stressors; the stuff we don't learn until we are in the throes of trauma. Some of us never learn them or take up unhealthy ones. The tips in the book can be applied to any life stressors or grief in many ways, some of which were mentioned already in the book like bankruptcy, divorce, job loss and many more. This book is a story of a true journey of hope through unimaginable grief. Not hope after grief. Not hope after loss. Not hope after stressors. Hope through these things. With these things. Cohesively living life with joy.

If you have a pool without a gate or you visit places with such risk, get your child swim lessons. They're never too young. Drownings can happen. They do happen. And they don't always happen to other people. Don't wait to get your child in swim lessons. Call today!

If you or someone you know is at risk for suicide or needs someone to talk to, please reach out thru the National Suicide Prevention Lifeline at 800-273-8255 or text HOME to 741741.

Continue to follow her journey as she delves into her next passion; proactive, non-clinical support groups for those at suicide risk. Her non-profit will be coming soon!

Contact info: jenny@suicideandsequins.com

Made in the USA
Middletown, DE
17 October 2022

12959288R00119